Timeless Books of Truth

When you're seeking a book on practical spiritual living, you want to know it's based on an authentic tradition of timeless teachings and resonates with integrity.

This is the goal of Crystal Clarity Publishers: to offer you books of practical wisdom filled with true spiritual principles that have not only been tested through the ages but also through personal experience.

Started in 1968, Crystal Clarity is the publishing house of Ananda, a spiritual community dedicated to meditation and living by true values, as shared by Paramhansa Yogananda and his direct disciple Swami Kriyananda, the founder of Ananda. The members of our staff and all of our authors live by these principles. Our work touches thousands around the world whose lives have been enriched by these universal teachings.

We publish only books that combine creative thinking, universal principles, and a timeless message. Crystal Clarity books will open doors to help you discover more fulfillment and joy by living and acting from the center of peace within you.

Meditation
for
Starters

Meditation
for
Starters

Swami Kriyananda

Crystal Clarity Publishers
Nevada City, California

Crystal Clarity Publishers, Nevada City, CA 95959
© 2008, 1996 by Hansa Trust
All rights reserved. Published 2008
First edition 1996. Second edition 2008

ISBN: 978-1-56589-229-3

Printed in Canada
10 9 8 7 6 5 4 3 2 1

Cover design and layout by Renee Glenn
Interior design and layout by Crystal Clarity

Library of Congress Cataloging-in-Publication Data
Walters, J. Donald.
  Meditation for Starters / by J. Donald Walters. — 2nd ed.
    p. cm.
  ISBN 978-1-56589-229-3 (trade paper)
  1. Meditation. I. Title.

BL627.W345 2008
204'.35—dc22

                                        2008014074

www.crystalclarity.com
clarity@crystalclarity.com
1-800-424-1055

Contents

Part I
The Way

Part II
Land of Mystery

PART ONE

❋

The Way

CHAPTER ONE

❄

Why Meditate?

Think how many things you do with the hope of attaining a condition of rest, once you've done them.

You think, "Let me buy that zippy red sports car, or that shiny white compact model, or that beautiful big station wagon for the whole family. I'll never rest until I get it!"

Or perhaps you think, "I'll get that new house with the shaded porch and the large master bedroom; that calm, spacious dining room so we don't have always to eat in the kitchen with the cucumbers; that sunken living room. Oh, once I have all that I'll be able to relax at last!"

Usually, our mental image of an attained ideal is like a framed painting: static and never changing. It is an end in itself, not a passageway toward further beginnings and further challenges. Even when we see our goals as means to other ends, our vision of the future carries us to a time where rest becomes truly possible at last.

Peace is the natural condition of the soul. People sometimes speak longingly of the peace of the grave—as in the term *"requiescat in pace"*—even if they imagine death as a descent into unconsciousness. The loss of consciousness itself seems to them, evidently, an attractive alternative to the ceaseless struggle of human existence. Meditation, however, poses an infinitely more attractive alternative, one that lifts the mind into a state of *superconscious* peace which, once attained, can be maintained through even the psychic upheaval of physical death.

Peace can never truly be found outside ourselves. What passes for peace is a temporary lull, merely, in the battle of life. That new car, once you've bought it, will be only a prelude to new pursuits and fresh challenges. That lovely home will turn out to be an invitation to new responsibilities, further involvements, and perhaps even stronger attachments.

What happens is that, in the process of pursuing one thing after another, forever in the hope of getting everything finally just the way you want it, you become accustomed to looking for things, for more and more ways of helping you to rest better. Someday, surely (you think), you'll be able to *enjoy* life completely. The irony is that, in the very process of pursuing rest, you gradually lose the ability to rest at all. And in the process of pursuing enjoyment, you lose the capacity really to enjoy anything.

Our very enjoyment of life begins with the simple ability to *relax*. The ability *is* simple: That is what makes it so difficult! Since our birth, our life-force has flowed outward to the five senses, and through them to this world of endless complexity. It isn't easy, now, to reverse that flow.

The more you seek rest through doing, the more restless you become. The more you seek happiness through the senses, the less happy you will be, for the simple reason that sensory enjoyment *drains* our capacity for happiness: It doesn't nourish it.

Why wait? Why wait for peace and happiness to come to you *eventually*? Will they come to you even after you retire from work? Hardly! If, having become safely ensconced in that rocking chair, you resist the tendency to keep on doing things no matter how unproductive, you'll very likely die of boredom.

Everyone, no matter how busy he is, needs to devote some time every day to practicing the art of *doing things restfully.* You'll never find peace *until you make peace a part of activity itself.* Peace should be part of the very creative process.

Hence the importance of meditation.

. . . . .

Questions and Answers

Question: *Are there other ways besides meditation to break a lifelong habit of restlessness?*

Answer: There are many ways. They are less direct, how-ever, because their focus is not so much on peace itself as on creating those conditions which will allow one to feel peaceful. Peace is not merely a passive state, experienced when the tur-moil around us has ceased.

People imagine they'll find peace in a peaceful setting—in that cottage by the sea to which they hope to retire; in that quiet life on a yacht. What they discover, if peace means to them a mere end to anxiety, is a life of steadily deepening ennui. True peace is never passive: It is dynamic. It emanates from a high level of awareness. It can be found only within, in the Self. Outward awareness, if over-stimulated, drains you of your peace; it can never *give* you peace.

It is good to prepare the ground for higher awareness, however, by simplifying one's life outwardly, and by reducing the quantity of your personal desires. It is important to hold an *attitude* of peacefulness. Without it, meditation will prove difficult for you.

At work, concentrate on doing one thing at a time. Finish one project before proceeding to the next one. Try not to "gobble" life. Move in an aura of calmness, and you'll find it easy to attain superconscious peace in meditation.

Question: *I find that in the welter of activity I become almost afraid of peace. Is there anything I can do to overcome this fear?*

Answer: This is one of the classic obstacles on the spiritual path: *false notion,* in the present case fearing the very thing you may desperately need and want.

The fear you mention is quite simply the consequence of physical and mental tension. If you fight that tension, you'll only become more tense. Concentrate first, therefore, on relaxation—physical, first, then mental. Later on, I'll go more deeply into the subject of relaxation and how it can be achieved.

Question: *You said at the end of the foregoing section that peace should be "part of the creative process." But isn't creativity very often the fruit of mental and emotional anguish, not of inner restfulness?*

Answer: It is, yes—but also, no, it isn't. Often it takes suffering to bring human consciousness to that level of maturity which produces deep insights. At the same time, a painting, for example, or a work of music cannot rightly be called "significant," what to speak of "great," if it only poses problems, and suggests no valid solutions to those problems.

In science and technology, creativity is measured not by the "Rube Goldberg"-like complexity of an invention, but by its workability. The simpler, indeed, the better. It is not enough for an inventor to pose a problem: To be hailed for his contribution to society, he must provide answers to that problem. Creativity of all kinds is not a labyrinthine wandering in search of a way out of difficulties: It is the glad cry, "*Eureka! I've found the exit.*"

Solutions are difficult to come by rationally. The reasoning mind is like a rudderless ship: It describes interesting patterns on the water, but it lacks a sure sense of direction. The rudder of inner guidance comes from superconscious levels of awareness.

On a personal note here, many years ago as a young man it was my ambition to be a playwright. Gratifyingly, a number of people in the theater predicted a bright future for me. (Theater people are notoriously lavish with their predictions.) After some time, however, I realized that, although I was perhaps traveling first class when it came to my awareness of life's problems, I was in steerage when it came to offering any answers. At some point, aware of the emotional anguish (as you put it in your question) of seeing only the problems, I decided that there was no point in flooding the world with my ignorance! Instead, I determined to devote my life to searching for answers. If ever I found a few, then, God willing, I would have something worthwhile to share with others.

And here is one truth of which I have become deeply convinced: No great work can ever be produced without at least a touch of superconscious inspiration. Such inspiration comes only—however fleetingly—in a state of inner peace, the peace that is attained most directly through meditation.

•　　•　　•　　•　　•

Visualization

Sit upright, and close your eyes. The following exercise will help to draw you into a meditative state.

Visualize yourself walking down a busy street in the center of a city. Crowds surge about you, each individual bent on some personal errand. The buildings around you hold countless other people, each one busily occupied in filing office papers, telephoning, issuing or acting upon important directives, checking into or out of a hotel, packing or unpacking, writing a letter, reading a book—the myriad occupations, in short, of a busy metropolis.

Now, imagine that all these people are a part of your own "population" of thoughts. Each one acts out some particular desire, some tendency, some perhaps forgotten interest of yours that you may have been holding, if only subconsciously.

All together they form that vast territory of consciousness which is your own mind.

Gaze calmly at all this activity and ask yourself: "Is this really who I am? Is any of it what I really want from life? What could I possibly accomplish by endlessly pursuing so many diverse, even conflicting, goals and interests?"

Reflect on the sheer madness of becoming ever-increasingly enmeshed in the search for outward fulfillment. "Surely," you tell yourself, "there must be a better way!"

Continue your walk down the street. Gradually, the crowds become thinner, the buildings, lower and less imposing. Your sense of personal involvement is diminishing.

The crowded downtown area lies behind you now. The street has become quiet, the activity in the houses, subdued.

Follow the street as it leaves the city. Relish the fresh atmosphere of the countryside. "This peace," you tell yourself gratefully, "is what my heart truly wants."

Enjoy that feeling of release from endless involvement in worldly ambitions and desires.

CHAPTER TWO

✳

What Is Meditation?

Meditation, properly speaking, begins once the thoughts and emotions have been stilled. It is a state of intense inward awareness, a state in which one's attention is no longer engaged in cheering onward the parade that life marches past us of projects and problems, but is wholly engrossed in the superconscious experience. Meditation may be defined also, more loosely, as any practice of which the goal is superconscious awareness.

For there are three states of consciousness: not only conscious and subconscious (about which most people know at least something), but also superconscious (about which few people know anything).

The conscious mind is our normal waking state of awareness. It represents only a small part of our total consciousness. A far larger part of it lies in the subconscious.

The subconscious, popularized in modern times by Sigmund Freud, is the hidden but often dominant part of our psyche. We experience something of the subconscious during sleep. The subconscious is active also during our wakeful hours; it influences our behavior, our very attitudes toward life. The subconscious is like the vast ocean with its floor of mountains, valleys, and broad plains. Conscious awareness protrudes from this ocean like a little island. Invisible to the island dweller is the great underwater region around him: the innumerable habits, tendencies, and unformed impressions that underlie the conscious mind. They represent a dimmer, but nonetheless very real, part of our total awareness.

The superconscious, by contrast, represents a much higher degree of awareness. Indeed, it is the true source of all awareness. The conscious and subconscious minds filter that higher awareness, merely—stepping it down, so to speak, like the transformer that converts a high voltage to a lower and makes it available to our homes.

Superconsciousness may be compared to the infinite sky overhead, with its vast panoply of stars. We know that the stars are always there, shining. We can only see them, however, when the sunlight doesn't fill the sky and obscure them. The sunlight, in this analogy, represents ego-generated thoughts and feelings, which blot superconscious awareness out of our mental sky. That superconsciousness is always with us, however. It is simply not dynamic to our normal waking consciousness.

Superconsciousness is situated, as the name implies, *above* our normal state of wakefulness. From that higher level come our occasional deep insights and inspirations, when our minds are in a calm and uplifted state. Those insights may penetrate the light of ego-wakefulness like brilliant comets, which have sometimes been seen in the sky even in bright daylight.

The superconscious is the realm of true vision. It contains the ecstasy experienced during periods of intense prayer or inward upliftment, when the ego's restlessness has been temporarily stilled.

The conscious mind, dependent on the intellect, seeks reasonable solutions to its problems. The subconscious mind influences the intellect by prompting it with deep-seated feelings, habit patterns, and personal tendencies. (Our conscious decisions are never so independent as we like to believe them!) Harmful habits, though difficult to banish from the mind, can—by repeated, conscious effort—be redirected into positive channels.

The direct way to attune ourselves to superconsciousness is by meditation. The essential attitude for correct meditation is one of *listening*. The difference between prayer and meditation is that in prayer we talk to God, whereas in meditation we listen for His answer.

In meditation, the mind must be kept *receptive*. You can't *think* your way into deep meditation. Nor, indeed, can you think your way to deep insights and inspirations. You can only receive wisdom: You cannot *concoct* it. A truth must be perceived, in that calm awareness which is superconsciousness.

Meditation, then, is not creating answers: It is perceiving, or *receiving* them. And this is the secret of creativity.

Meditation is listening. The mind must suspend its normal activity of analyzing, of weighing alternatives, and of generally "talking" so much that one cannot hear melodies that the super-conscious is playing to it.

Meditation is a process of returning to your own center. It is learning to relate to life and to your environment from who *you* are, and not from the way other people try to define you.

The average person's life is an eccentric flywheel. I don't mean a flywheel with an offbeat personality! I mean simply a flywheel that isn't properly centered. The faster the wheel turns, the more violently it vibrates. When it reaches a certain speed, it may actually fly into pieces.

Most people, similarly, are in danger of flying apart. They whirl through life, vibrating ever more violently because they are off center within. It is safe to say that few people live even close to their center, which is who they really are! They live at their periphery. They are constantly, as the popular expression puts it, "on edge."

Again, most people are like out-of-tune musical instruments. Because they can no longer hear the basic notes in themselves, their interactions with life and with other people produce only discords.

Meditation is the way to "fine tune" your instrument. A violinist, while tuning his strings, must listen carefully to certain key notes. We, too, must listen to what life is trying to tell us—through outer circumstances and through other people, as well as through the whispers of superconsciousness.

Daily meditation will lead you to the peace you've been seeking so long. The peace of your soul awaits you at the center of your own being.

How much or how long you meditate is up to you. It depends on how deeply you've come to enjoy the practice. We aren't talking, here, of a roast in the oven which requires a certain baking time. And we aren't talking of distances—like a mile run, which can be finished sooner by running faster. I *do* suggest that you make meditation a daily practice. That, too, however, is up to you.

The more regularly and the more deeply you meditate, the sooner you will find yourself acting always from a center of inner peace.

• • • • •

Questions and Answers

Question: *Is meditation "listening" to anything, specifically? Or is it simply a mental attitude of receptivity, for which listening is only a metaphor?*

Answer: I use the word literally as well as metaphorically. Metaphorically, it describes, as you suggest, an attitude of openness and receptivity. Literally, however, there are actual sounds heard in deep meditation that emanate from the superconscious, and that help to raise the consciousness to ever higher levels.

There are also subtle lights seen in meditation, refined feelings experienced, and deep intuitions of wisdom, love, and joy. I go into these points at length in another book of mine, *Awaken to Superconsciousness—A Guide to Meditation,* published by Crystal Clarity in California.

Question: *In what way is meditation different from self-hypnosis?*

Answer: Hypnosis opens the mind *downward*; it increases our susceptibility to subconscious influences. Both hypnosis and self-hypnosis can be helpful for working on those influences and changing them if they are harmful. Neither form of hypnosis, however, improves discrimination, which descends from a level of superconscious awareness.

What hypnosis does is blur the threshold between conscious and subconscious awareness. It makes the conscious mind, in turn, more susceptible to subconscious influences in general. The long-range effect of both hypnosis and self-hypnosis, therefore, is to weaken the will power. This effect is particularly insidious if one allows oneself to be repeatedly hypnotized by other persons.

Consciously directed affirmations to the subconscious, on the other hand, produce positive results, particularly when they are then offered upward to the superconscious. For self-transformation occurs, finally, when the resolution to change is charged with superconscious awareness, and thence fully absorbed into the subconscious.

Question: *You've mentioned the need for "tuning" oneself. How does meditation bring about attunement?*

Answer: In clarifying the mind it also clarifies our conscious directions. We live so to speak in a world of mirrors. Each of us sees reflected back to him from the world the energies and attitudes that are first projected by himself. When we are angry, we see ample support everywhere for our anger. When we are peaceful, we see positive reinforcement in everything for our peacefulness.

Much of the disharmony we experience is due simply to the fact that our desires are in conflict with one another. Singlemindedness is a rare virtue. People may want success, but fear the effort necessary to succeed. They may want popularity, but fear to put themselves out to be liked; or they may want popularity, yet have an equally strong liking for solitude. They may want love, but fear to give love lest they be hurt in return. They may desire to travel, but fear the uncertainties involved in leaving home.

"The thwarting crosscurrents," as Paramhansa Yogananda called them, of egoic desire are so complex that it is hardly surprising how few people achieve more than fleeting glimpses of inner peace.

Daily meditation gradually smooths out the tangle. It brings the separate strands of desire into alignment with one another and enables them finally to focus on a single objective at a time—as a thread, after it has been brought to a point, is easily inserted through the eye of a needle.

•　　•　　•　　•　　•

Visualization

(Continued from Chapter 1)

Leave behind you the city with its preoccupations and worries. The street you've followed into the quiet outskirts of the city now winds through peaceful countryside. Grassy meadows on either side of the road reveal gay sweeps of colored flowers between gaps in the high hedges. A stand of oak trees looms proudly on a far knoll, their limbs stretched out in greeting to the land. Nearby, a forest calls to you: "Enter, friend. Forsake your memories of your concrete jungle in our quiet, tree-lined aisles. Discover here something that your harried life has so far denied you!"

Flocks of birds fly overhead, their flight an image of restful symmetry. Listen! They call to you as they pass overhead: "Fly with us in spirit—high, ever higher, to distant lands, to sunny climes and perfect happiness!"

Smaller birds chirp to you merrily in the bushes. Songbirds in the trees thrill the air with sweet melodies, their notes wafted over the meadows on gentle breezes. And the breezes themselves play lightly among the meadow grasses, producing delightful harmonies.

And then—whence comes it? You know not!—a shepherd's pipe calls to you in the distance.

Behind, in that all-but-forgotten city, throbs a life of fretful striving and desires. Here, you are surrounded by high thoughts and aspirations. The flower-strewn meadows, the sturdy oak trees, the silently beckoning forest, the birds in flight above your head and their tuneful brothers and sisters close by, the happy breezes, the shepherd's pipe—all the sounds and sights of a harmonious countryside symbolize your inner self, your thoughts, feelings, and aspirations. Noble ideals arise spontaneously in your mind, once the city's preoccupations have ceased to importune you.

Listen intently to the sounds around you. Concentrate on them, each one in turn.

Now, perceive in them the combined symphony of your longing for a better life. Let your spirits soar upward and outward in pure love and joy. These, you tell yourself, are the true, the long-sought keys to earthly perfection.

CHAPTER THREE

※

How to Meditate?

The first thing you need for correct meditation is a right mental attitude, particularly, as I've said, one of *listening*.

Most people seldom listen. They are deaf to the symphony of sounds in the world around them. They are deaf to other people, for they are more interested in speaking their own minds. They treat their own conscience as though it were a defect to be overcome. They behave as though perpetually campaigning for their own ideas. Like bettors at a horse race, they keep *willing* the "right" horse to win.

The process is never-ending. Every horizon reached, if it ever *is* reached, only opens up new vistas of expectation and of wishful thinking. Some people, when a particularly cherished hope ends, live out the rest of their lives in a wonderful dream-world of Might-Have-Been.

For a few minutes every day, why not give this process a rest? Stop decreeing your opinions to the universe. There is a state of awareness that precedes the very process of thinking. Seek that. It lies in inner calmness. Granted, this state isn't easy to find. One thing that will help you to find it, however, is *listening*.

Listen to your thoughts. Listen to what *is;* don't keep on insisting on what you think *ought* to be. Tune in to things as they are. Train your mind to accept what simply *is*.

Meditation is the opposite of imposing your will on the world. Relinquish, even for just a few minutes, the process of concocting plans and projects for the future. Be more, not less, conscious, however. Just as I suggested that you act calmly, so also, during moments of calmness, be *dynamically aware*.

In dawning calmness you may find yourself, at first, tempted to drift off passively into a sort of semi-subconscious state. There is a certain restfulness in this state, as there is in sleep. It is a temporary rest, however; it doesn't refresh the spirit. Nor has it power to improve your life, as superconsciousness has. Subconsciously induced rest lowers your level of energy and will power, and makes you subject to conditions over which you ought to be gaining mastery. It takes a strong will, generating great energy, to rise above, or even to calm, life's storms.

Don't seek peace as a certain woman did, of whom it was said after her husband died, "She's taking it beautifully. Her doctor gave her tranquilizers, and she hardly realizes what's happened to her." There is neither victory nor any long-term emotional reprieve in relative unconsciousness.

The calmness born of deep meditation represents a higher degree of awareness, and therefore of will and energy, than any experienced in lower states. Meditation-born calmness will enable you not only to remain calm during periods of intense activity, but also to face, and accept with wise understanding, the trials of life.

Your goal, then, should at all times be to remain "*actively calm, and calmly active.*"

To develop inner calmness, *listen* intently to the silence within. Listening in this context is another word for being fully aware—for not drifting mentally, but soaring upward to greater heights of awareness.

There is no limit to the heights attainable in superconsciousness. This state is natural to everyone, though few have ever explored it. (As Sri Krishna said in the Indian scripture the *Bhagavad Gita*, "Out of a thousand, one seeks Me.") Many have had glimpses of superconsciousness, however, during moments of inner stillness, or during sleep. Meditation is a means of attuning the mind to superconsciousness, and, in time, of entering that state. All that is needed, to bring that level of awareness to you, is to disperse the fog of mental restlessness.

Superconsciousness is that aspect of the mind which is attuned to the great flow of life. To attain superconsciousness, it will help you to know that it has a specific seat in the brain. That seat is located in the frontal lobe, behind the forehead, at a point midway between the eyebrows. By gazing up toward that point, and by lifting your concentration there in a state of deep calmness and relaxation, you will become fully aware, in time, of that highest aspect of your being.

Listening involves, as I have pointed out, a mental attitude of *receptivity*. The more deeply and consciously receptive you become, the deeper and more satisfying will your meditations be. By receptivity, you will begin to understand your connection to all Life. For human beings are like ripples on the great ocean of existence. Our appearance of separateness is an illusion, merely, produced by ego-consciousness, and reinforced by our attachment to little preoccupations.

The child playing with its toys, the woman weeping over a recent death, the young lovers skipping playfully on a beach, the old man nodding on a park bench, caressing his memories: All these are a part of *your own* greater reality!

You are not just Joe or Sally Green with a porch to fix, a refrigerator to stock up for the weekend, an apartment to tidy, children to get off to school, or a business contract to prepare. You are *all* these people and many more.

In your greater reality, you are the ocean of Life itself!

By receptivity of feeling and sympathy, as well as of thought, you will develop intuition, the hallmark of superconscious living.

Listen, therefore. Be receptive. *Be relaxed*. Without relaxation—of mind as well as of body—you won't be able to concentrate deeply. And you won't ever become truly receptive.

• • • • •

Questions and Answers

Question*: Is there anything you can suggest for helping me to become more aware of my thoughts as I meditate?*

Answer: The important thing is not to become caught up in them. Don't be like the weak swimmer who gets swept away by a strong river current. Stand mentally on the bank, and watch the current flow past you. Be calmly observant of the flow, mentally detached from it.

Imagine that the bank on which you stand is situated at the back of your head, in the region of the medulla oblongata. There in fact lies the seat of ego-consciousness. From that position, watch your thoughts and feelings flowing by you. Realize, as you watch, that not only your thoughts but your very perception of what is important keeps passing. Nothing in life, neither your inner thoughts nor your outer circumstances, is firmly fixed. If any thought, feeling, or circumstance seems permanent to you, it is only because it has become snagged, temporarily, on a protruding rock of attachment. In a spirit of freedom, allow the current to release it from the rock. Behold that object of attachment sweeping onward again.

Gradually detach your feelings from the ceaseless flow. Gaze calmly at the opposite bank. And consider that bank to be situated at the seat of superconsciousness, the point between your eyebrows. Reach out beyond it, to a land of freedom from all earthly problems—of permanent escape from "all the misbelieving and black horde"* of delusion.

Question: *Would it help if I also listened to the river?*

Answer: Indeed, yes. In this book I've used the word *listening* partly to increase your sense of total absorption in meditation. Don't only watch the river: *Listen* to it. Hear its ripples against the bank. Smell its water. Taste the water, even. Make the experience of the river as real to your imagination as possible.

Question: *But is it actually good to imagine things? Isn't there a danger, in doing so, of deluding oneself? I wonder whether a risk in meditating isn't that we may invite false images to arise in the mind from the subconscious, and to*

---

* From the *Rubaiyat of Omar Khayyam*, Paramhansa Yogananda wrote a brilliant and wise explanation of this ancient poem, showing its deep mystical meaning. This book, titled *The Rubaiyat of Omar Khayyam Explained*, is published by Crystal Clarity Publishers.

masquerade as reality. Hallucinations, I suspect, come more readily when the mind is calm. Isn't that, indeed, an advantage of the very state you've cautioned us against: restlessness?

Answer: You have a point! One of the obstacles on the path of meditation is listed by Patanjali, who for thousands of years has been the recognized authority on yoga, as "false visions."

The problem, however, lies not with the imagination itself. The imaginative faculty can be a priceless aid toward spiritual attainment, as it is toward every kind of creativity. The problem, rather, lies with an *undisciplined* imagination.

The conscious mind is constantly influenced by the subconscious. It is *even more* influenced when the mind is restless. For although its attention may not be sharply focused enough to clothe its fears and longings in hallucinatory forms, there is no doubt that it conjures up constant reminders of ideas for which there is no reasonable basis. Those reminders rise to a conscious level from the subconscious. People imagine they detect malice in an innocuous statement, or the certainty of failure in a temporary setback. If the conscious mind is passively open to suggestions, it is easily influenced, and not always constructively so. If it drifts idly during meditation, as it may easily do when the will is not actively engaged, images may appear to the consciousness that are purely subjective, and not superconscious at all. This process is a sort of conscious dreaming. By developing the imagination actively, however, the conscious mind is kept more dynamically aware. Thus, control is gained over the suggestive power of the subconscious mind.

Artistic expression, too, can be a way of "taming" the subconscious mind. The important thing is that the artist take control, and not merely open his conscious mind to suggestions from the subconscious. The method is simple: Hold up *to the superconscious* any thought you want to give artistic form. Then invite the subconscious to interact with that higher inspiration.

Science has found that people who engage in any kind of creative activity actually develop their brains in the areas that are engaged during that activity. Composers and musicians develop the musical part of their brains; it isn't only that they owe their talent to the prior development of that region. Painters and sculptors, similarly, develop the visual areas of their brains.

It is possible to tell by looking at an artist whether his art is musical or visual. His energy seems to flow more toward the sense of hearing if he is a musician. If he is a painter, there will be evident an emphasis on the sense of sight. Jewelers, I've noticed, often have more-than-ordinarily bright eyes. Writers and composers may seem to focus their energy more on their *inner* sense of sight or of hearing.

Thus, visualizations that are focused on any aspect of the spiritual quest develop those corresponding areas of the brain. Visualizations, for example, that are directed toward the point between the eyebrows develop the frontal lobe of the brain in that particular area. The more you can hold your concentration there, the sooner true, superconscious experiences will come to you.

Question: *If I am not Joe or Sally Green, or whoever, why does it seem to me that my own body and personality so entirely define me as I am? Surely, were I to dissolve that identity, I would dissolve my very being—wouldn't I? How can I dissolve this brain and not lose consciousness altogether? Doesn't consciousness itself depend on the brain's activity?*

Answer: This is a great mistake modern people make, especially in science. Consciousness could not be *produced* by the brain any more than it can be produced by a computer, which is so often compared to the human brain in the way it functions. Rather, consciousness precedes the creation of both the brain and the body. It takes *consciousness* to think; it isn't thought that produces consciousness.

Consciousness precedes the manifestation of the ego, also. The reality of the soul is intrinsic to the reality of life. The soul is ever conscious. The ego, like a wave on the ocean's surface, is only a manifestation of the soul's deeper awareness. The ego was defined by Paramhansa Yogananda as "the soul identified with the body." The ego is transcended finally in a state of ecstasy. As Jesus Christ put it, "For whosoever will save his life shall lose it: but whosoever will lose his life for my sake, the same shall save it" (Luke 9:24). The consciousness of the little self, in other words, must be offered into an ever-expanding awareness of infinity. The incentive to martyrdom, which is how many early Christians read this passage, pales beside the call to total ego-transcendence. Self-realization is the conscious realization of oneness with the Source of life, which is infinite.

Question: *Is the ego, then, as many spiritual writers have claimed, our mortal enemy?*

Answer: It is our enemy, yes, but it is also our friend. Which it is depends on whether our aim in life is to expand our understanding, or to remain forever stuck at our present stage of spiritual evolution. If we embrace expansion toward ever broader realities, the ego is our friend, helping us to reach out to our true Self: the soul. If, on the other hand, we incline self-contractively toward pettiness and selfishness, the ego is our enemy, alienating us as it does from who we really are.

The soul, not the ego, is our true self. The soul is obscured, but it can never be destroyed, by worldly-mindedness. The ego has a choice: It can either embrace limitation, and consequent suffering, or it can reach out toward limitless freedom and joy.

*   *   *   *   *

Visualization

Continue the visualization you learned in the first two chapters.

Imagine yourself walking again upon that country road. Listen again to the birds' songs. Feel that all Nature is reflecting back to you your own soul's aspirations.

The road now descends, leading you eventually to a river bank. The river is too wide and deep to be crossed easily.

Stand there on the river bank, and watch the current flowing past you—whether swiftly or slowly depends on your own mental state. For the river, too, is a part of your own being. Its flow is the current of your own thoughts and feelings.

Gaze across the river. See there, interrupted for now, the next stage of your journey. A road on the other side leads away invitingly toward a brilliant sunset in the distance, radiating golden light above soaring mountain peaks. Your heart calls you there. For you see there a land of peace, of eternal freedom from former bondage and pain.

Standing on the near bank, feel that your position there is located at the back of your head, in the region of the medulla oblongata at the base of the brain. That land of freedom beyond lies past the point between your eyebrows. The river flows through the middle of your brain, between those two regions. Gaze at the land on the other side of the river; be only mildly aware of the water's flow, between. Don't identify yourself too closely with that which forever passes.

You know, somehow, that you must pass over that river of ego-motivated thoughts and feelings. How can you do it?

One way would be to watch with calm, inner detachment as, gradually, the river dries up, for you are not supplying it anymore with water. When the bed is dry, you'll be able simply to walk across it.

You can also, with a mighty will, put out strong energy to divide the water, leaving a clear passageway for you to walk across.

Meanwhile, rid your mind of the flow of impeding thoughts and feelings. There must be no remaining obstacles to your progress toward soul-freedom.

CHAPTER FOUR

❄

Preparation for Meditation

It is important to prepare oneself properly for meditation. If you try meditating after a hearty meal, for example, your energy will be working hard, meanwhile, to digest that food. For it is the same energy your body uses for digestion as your mind uses to concentrate deeply. If the energy is diverted to your stomach, you will have less for effective meditation.

Just try talking abstract philosophy after a heavy meal. You'll miss some of the fine points of the discussion; or you may find ideas slipping away just as you reach out to grab them. If you force yourself to concentrate, you may get indigestion as a result of forcibly redirecting your energy to the brain.

Before meditating, eat only lightly. Better still, don't eat at all: Wait two or three hours, in other words, after a full meal.

The best hours for meditation are—taking only your own convenience into consideration—when you wake up in the morning, before meals, and at night just before going to bed.

Those considerations aside, there are also universally good times for meditation, unrelated to personal schedules. These times are, roughly, at 6 a.m., 12 noon, 6 p.m., and midnight: hours related to the sun's movement. Because this movement varies, the recommendations themselves are only general. To be more specific, the best morning and afternoon hours are at sunrise and at sunset.

These four times are recommended particularly because they correspond to changing energies in the earth's atmosphere. There occurs at each of these shifts a "rest point" in Nature. It is rather like the pause that occurs when a ball is tossed up into the air, just before it begins its descent. By meditating at, or near, these rest points in Nature you will find it easier to achieve mental calmness.

If these classically recommended times don't suit your daily schedule, however, don't worry about it. The benefit of meditating at Nature-ordained hours is secondary to the importance of meditation itself. Simply choose times, in this case, that are personally suitable to you. But I do make one strong suggestion: Try to *meditate at the same times* every day. In that way you'll develop habit patterns that will make it increasingly easier to put aside distracting thoughts when you sit for meditation.

The atmospheric energies mentioned above are subtle, but are nonetheless real. You may become aware of them as meditation helps you to develop sensitivity.

Many societies have, in one way and another, emphasized the importance of attuning oneself with the earth's energies. Some of these societies have been what many Westerners today consider "primitive." (Isn't it arrogance, really, that labels any society primitive? I'm reminded of a question someone posed to Mahatma Gandhi. "What do you think," the visitor asked, "of Western civilization?" Wryly the Indian leader replied, "I think it would be a good idea!") Other more "acceptably" advanced civilizations have taken the subtle earth energies quite seriously. I've gone into this rather theoretical aspect of the subject at some length in my book *Awaken to Superconsciousness* (Crystal Clarity Publishers).

There are other energies than those in the atmosphere. Some of them—I'm not speaking here of the force of gravity— act upon the life-force in the body to draw it downward.

In meditation, you see, the life-force needs to flow toward the brain. You can insulate yourself against certain of those downward-pulling energies. The insulation need not be some "cutting-edge" electronic device. A simple woolen blanket will do. A deer skin is even more effective. Sit on either of these during meditation. Even if you don't experience these benefits consciously, take it on faith from people whose consciousness, developed through years of meditation, has become finely tuned to the earth energies. The ability of yogis to make such observations is as matter-of-fact as yours would be in telling some hermit in the Himalaya how to position a TV antenna to get the best reception.

An insulation with even greater results would be to place a silk cloth over your woolen blanket or deer skin.

The direction you face in meditation also affects concentration. Again, time of day, insulation, direction—none of these is *essential*. They are aids, simply.

If, then, you find it convenient to do so, sit facing east. If east is not convenient, owing to the layout of your home, face north.

Enlightenment, according to numerous ancient traditions, comes to us from the east. I don't mean from the Orient, but from a direction east of wherever one happens to be.

According to certain ancient traditions, spiritual liberation comes, similarly, from the north. Since our concern is with attaining freedom from bondage to ego-involvement, it would be interesting to consider the northern direction from this point of view. At the time of death, for instance, yogis consider it helpful to point the head northward. When a person wants to meditate on freeing himself from worldly concerns, it is good, again, to face north.

Try weighing those claims in light of what you yourself know of life, and of history. Doesn't the flow of civilization seem, indeed, to have been westward? And doesn't a greater spirit of freedom seem to flow downward from the north? This seems to me to be true in every country, though I haven't made an exhaustive study of the matter. The spirit of orthodoxy, on the other hand, and of faithfulness to tradition, seems to flow northward from the southern part of every country.

These phenomena manifest themselves variously. The desire for freedom, for example, may express itself in ways as varied as a spirit of rebellion, in some people, and a yearning for

release from spiritual bondage, in others. The spirit of orthodoxy may find expression in ways as diverse as dogmatic resistance to improvement, and, in other people, loyalty to values
which, tested over centuries, have been found to be true.

In meditation, the spiritual aspirant normally seeks both
enlightenment (the energy from the east) and soul-freedom
(the energy from the north). A westward direction is for giving, rather than for receiving, energy. In meditation one should
seek to receive rather than to give (except, of course, if one
chooses, to share with others, later, the fruits of meditation).
East, then, is the proper direction for meditation.

Again, a southern direction is adapted to affirming the sta-
tus quo, not to rebelling against it. Meditation, on the contrary,
calls for inner release from egoic patterns of thinking. North,
then, is a better direction for meditators than south.

The question remains: Which is best for meditation—east,
or north? Enlightenment must come before liberation can be
attained. East, therefore, is the preferred direction for the seeker.
North is still good, however, if the position of your meditation
area makes it preferable.

If you can set aside a special place for meditation, do so.
Best, to be sure, would be a room wholly dedicated to medita-

tion, but if that isn't possible then you could simply screen off a portion of your bedroom. Such a space will enable you to build up meditative vibrations in it. After some time, you will feel the calmness the moment you enter there.

What about posture? Is one position best for meditation?

You might imagine that the most relaxed position would be lying flat on your back. Well, it might be the most relaxed, but it would not be the most conducive to meditation. The problem with a supine position is that it makes it easier to slip into subconsciousness. Meditation should carry you into the superior peace of superconsciousness.

In the Western church of Christianity, the traditional posture for prayer and worship is kneeling. In the Eastern Orthodox Church, people pray and worship standing up. Kneeling helps to induce a spirit of humility. Standing demonstrates formal respect for the Lord. The problem with both positions, for meditation, is that they are not aids to relaxation. In meditation you want to rise above body-consciousness. To be tense is to be body-bound.

There is no point, moreover, in trying to impress God with your humility or with your awe before Him. He knows every ripple of your heart's feelings. Before Him you can hide nothing.

To forget yourself, then, is humility enough. Indeed, the best
definition of humility is complete self-forgetfulness. And
the best expression of respect is to become absorbed in con-
templating Him.

For humility is not self-abasement, as many people
imagine. It is rising above the little self in surrender to God's
infinite love and wisdom. Worshipers who bow to the ground
ritualistically again and again, and who figuratively throw dust
on their own heads, too often ignore God while paying such
exaggerated attention to their own unworthiness.

Are we truly nothing before God? If so, why not stop
thinking about this "nothing" and give ourselves to Him
entirely? It is often in their outward show of humility that
people most surely express pride.

There is a story, told to me by a Jewish friend, of a rabbi who,
one Saturday in the synagogue, went before the altar, threw himself on his knees, and cried loudly, "I'm nothing! I'm nothing!"

The assistant rabbi, inspired by this show of humility, followed suit. He, too, threw himself on his knees and shouted,
"I'm nothing! I'm nothing!"

At this point the janitor, moved by their example, rushed down the aisle, cast himself also on his knees before the altar, and cried, "I'm nothing! I'm nothing!"

The rabbi, with a quizzical expression, turned to his assistant and said, "So look who thinks he's nothing!"

Meditation is usually practiced as an act of worship, but it needn't be. Its real purpose is to help us to realize on ever deeper levels of our being who we really are, in our deepest nature. If to you this quest means plumbing your ego to its depths, then an attitude of worship may be unnecessary. If, however, you think of God alone as your true Self, worship will come naturally to you. In either case, the deeper you penetrate to the heart of truth, the more spontaneously will feelings of worship arise inside you. For the truth of who you are, behind your ego, is awe-inspiring. At present, however, you may want simply to find peace of mind. In that case, this, too, is meditation. The important thing is to become inwardly calm. And the first step toward inner calmness is utter relaxation.

The best posture, then, for achieving this condition is the one recommended in the East: seated.

Whether you sit on the floor in a traditional cross-legged position, or even on a chair, is not greatly important. There are certain advantages to sitting cross-legged. The lotus pose, for example, and some of the other positions traditionally recommended in the yoga teachings, exert pressure on certain nerves and thereby help to induce physical relaxation. The disadvantage to these positions, for many Westerners, is that their bodies are accustomed to sitting in chairs. Relaxation, when their legs are bent in seemingly impossible pretzel shapes, is not only difficult, but, for many of them, impossible. The question of rising above body-consciousness becomes moot for them. Instead of asking themselves, "When will my spirit soar?" they wonder desperately, "Will I ever walk again?"

In fact, only two things are necessary: that the spine be kept straight, and the body, relaxed. A straight spine is important for two reasons: First, it induces a positive mental attitude, and second, it makes it easier for the life-force to flow toward the brain. So then—sit on a chair if you prefer, but in any case, keep your spine straight.

If you sit on a chair, choose one that is armless. The woolen blanket (and the silk cloth, if you use it to cover the blanket) should descend over the back of the chair, over the seat, and down under your feet.

Place your hands palms upward on the thighs, at the junction of the abdomen.

Keep your elbows back, your shoulder blades drawn slightly together, and your chest up. All the while, emphasize relaxation; don't be tense.

Hold the chin slightly back, parallel to the ground.

Look upward, and close your eyes.

In the next chapter we'll consider more specifically *how* to relax the body.

•　　•　　•　　•　　•

Questions and Answers

Question: *You mentioned "rest points." Are there such points also in the way the body functions, comparable to those in objective Nature?*

Answer: There are, of course, for we are inextricably a part of Nature. That is why we resonate with outer events in Nature. Between every breath, for instance, and the next there is a rest point. A rest point occurs between the exhalation and the inhalation, and again between the inhalation and the exhalation. You will find it a good practice to watch the breath during meditation. Concentrate especially on those pauses between the breaths. Enjoy them.

Be aware also of the pauses at other rest points in your life: at the end of a sequence of thoughts or of feelings; at the moment of a shift in your activities; at the moment of waking or of going to sleep. Learn to live more at these pauses. Don't drown your awareness in a vortex of constant activity.

A good technique for changing directions in your life that you don't like—a bad mood, for example, or a fit of jealousy, anger, or despair—is deliberately to create a pause, both physically and mentally—then use that pause to affirm the change you want. Here's how to do it:

Inhale, and tense the body; throw the breath out, and relax. Then hold the breath out for as long as you find it comfortable to do so, Keep the mind free from all thoughts for the time being. When you need to inhale again, inhale with the breath the thought of an opposite energy to the one you want to change. At the same time, fill your mind with happy and constructive thoughts: kindness and acceptance toward all, if your problem is jealousy; calm non-attachment and good humor, if it is anger; courage, if it is despair. And so on.

* * * * *

Visualization

Continue the visualization we've followed so far. Stand on the river bank. Look across at the other side, and prepare yourself for the crossing, still sensing, at the back of your brain, the need to calm those currents of ego-involvement, of restless thoughts, feelings, and desires.

Now, reach out mentally to the world around you. Sense its subtle energy-influences and the ways in which they affect you. Draw on energies that are beneficial. Protect yourself from those that are harmful, by mentally enclosing yourself in a sphere of light. Chant mentally, "I am light! I am peace! I am love! Radiant light alone, peace alone, love alone touch me and make me whole."

Meditate on the thought of the protective divine power, surrounding and embracing you.

CHAPTER FIVE

❈

Relaxing the Body

The best way to relax the body is to tense it first, and thereby to equalize the flow of tension all over the body. Then, with relaxation, you will find tensions being released that you didn't even know existed.

This method works also in the case of emotional tension. Often, emotional release comes only after an emotion has reached a peak of intensity. Prior to that intensity, the emotion may not have become clearly enough defined to you for it to be fully understood for what it is.

Psychological flaws, too, are difficult to address as long as they are sustained by one-horsepower energy in the mind. A person may seem quite innocuous, until good health, and a renewal of energy, brings out a mean streak that always lurked inside him.

Spiritual tests and trials are a blessing, in the sense that they help to bring a kind of tension to our flaws, and thereby heighten our awareness of them. The calm acceptance that heralds the passing of a test is often accompanied by a release of the flaw itself.

For physical relaxation, then, necessary as it is for deep meditation, first tense then relax the entire body.

To begin with, take a few slow, deep breaths in order to free the blood stream of any excessive build-up of carbon. If time permits, practice the following exercise:

1) Inhale, counting mentally to 12.

2) Hold the breath, counting to 12.

3) Exhale, again counting to 12.

Repeat this process 6–12 times. Then inhale deeply and tense the whole body, not suddenly, but smoothly: low, medium, high. Tense hard enough to vibrate the body. Then throw the breath out quickly and release the tension all over the body. Repeat this process once or twice more.

From now on, it will be important to keep your body motionless. You may find it difficult to sit perfectly still, at first, accustomed as you may be to moving constantly. The moment you decide to sit still, you may find yourself wanting to fidget! The longer you can hold your body completely still, however, the easier it will be to continue doing so. Your physical restlessness will vanish after five minutes or so. Soon you'll find yourself enjoying this sense of freedom from body-consciousness.

Remember, to be muscle-bound is to be a slave to the body. Dump the body, mentally, and dwell on the thought of space.

Visualize yourself surrounded by space—space all around you; space slowly entering your body through the pores of your skin like a vapor of pure light; space permeating your body, bringing it total relaxation.

Check yourself mentally every now and then, to make sure your body is still relaxed. If you feel tension anywhere, concentrate there especially, and visualize space, or pure light, in that region. Or, if your body is becoming generally tense, inhale again, tense the whole body, then throw the breath out and relax.

Psychological relaxation too is important. You can't meditate deeply—in fact, you can't really meditate at all—if you are mentally tense. Among the main causes of psychological tension are feelings of hostility and competitive anger, and the desire to exert power in some way over other people or over objective circumstances.

For mental relaxation, focus your attention in the heart. Imagine there a pure, white light. Visualize that light flowing outward in rays of love and harmony to the world around you. The heart is the center of emotional feeling. If the emotions are kept generous and calm, they develop into intuition, bringing an expansion of inner freedom. But if they are selfish or disturbed, they will produce only confusion and a feeling of inner bondage.

For most people, the energy flowing outward from their hearts has the effect of enmeshing them in things, in circumstances, and in the lives of others. Such people are filled with desires and aversions, either clutching at other rays of energy to possess them, or else doing battle with them in the hope of subduing or overwhelming them.

Imagine in your heart, instead, a kindly light. Send that light outward in rays of blessing to all. Mentally bless everyone near you; then, from your heart, send blessings to people in all lands, everywhere. Send rays of love to all creatures, to all things. Bless the rocks, the deserts, the vast oceans and high mountains. Surround the entire world in an aura of light, love, and joy. For everything is alive. All beings, all things manifest consciousness in varying degrees. They are part of the same eternal life that animates you.

You will feel blessed, yourself, and filled with inner peace, the more you offer yourself in service as a channel of peace and blessings to all.

•　•　•　•　•

Questions and Answers

Question: *You've mentioned the blessing of spiritual tests. (Most of us would put that word* blessing *in quotes!) What is the best way of meeting those tests? If concentrating on increasing the tension in the body, before releasing it altogether, is the best way to relax the body, is the best way of overcoming tests to concentrate on the tension they create?*

Should we emphasize our emotional suffering, for example, as a prelude to dismissing it completely? Again, should we heighten our feeling of guilt over some spiritual flaw, prior to freeing ourselves from it altogether?

Answer: This point is important. An increase of suffering may indeed be necessary, sometimes, as a means of helping us to overcome the cause of that particular suffering altogether. Yet, there is a difference between suffering and sorrow—between the experience itself, in other words, and whatever mental distress arises in response to that experience.

The right spiritual attitude toward suffering of any kind is mental detachment. Better still, add to that detachment the ingredient of love. Love will help you to rise above suffering altogether.

On no account surrender yourself to the pain you feel. For by surrender you'll only increase its power over you. You won't decrease it. Yes, that bit of bad karma will exhaust itself in time, but the delusion that first created it will remain entrenched, and will sprout, seedlike, to produce new suffering. People, again, who think to overcome anger by first intensifying it—perhaps even by screaming and hurling objects at a wall—may exhaust the mood temporarily, but in fact they only affirm anger to the subconscious. No release can come through negative affirmations.

Even during the tension that precedes deep physical relaxation, the mind should remain calm. It should not be tensed. Otherwise, the relaxation will be only momentary. Tension will flood the body anew, as the mind rethinks its position and decides that it can't relax after all. When tensing the body prior to relaxing it, center your concentration in the medulla oblongata at the base of the brain. Gaze from that point toward the seat of will power and enlightenment between the eyebrows. Let your subsequent relaxation release the energy to flow toward that point.

The way to overcome spiritual tests, then, is to remain peaceful. "Tests," Paramhansa Yogananda said, "should be faced calmly, with a pleasant attitude."

Good comes not from emotional intensity, but from the calmness that ensues from seeing an emotion steadily, and—as the saying goes—seeing it whole. The sooner calmness comes, the sooner the flaw is overcome. That is one reason why real changes in human nature come primarily from contact with superconsciousness.

Question: *You tell us to relax deeply. Yet at the same time you emphasize being dynamically aware. To be dynamically* *aware implies, to my mind, the use of will power. And to use will power implies effort. How can we resolve the conflict between "trying hard" and not, simultaneously, becoming tensed?*

Answer: It is important to distinguish between *tense* effort (an attitude engendered by outward striving) and absorption in ever deeper relaxation. Will power is necessary, but the will must be exerted in the beginning toward deepening the enjoyment of relaxation.

Question: *Is there any way of increasing my awareness of an emotion, as a means of releasing it altogether?*

Answer: You must take care not to affirm its reality, through your awareness of it. What you *can* do is diminish your sense of its reality by observing it with calm detachment. Don't affirm its reality for you, personally.

Then bring clarity to that observation by imagining the emotion in its extreme form. Visualize its harmful effect on yourself and on others. Visualize how it distorts your ability to understand anything clearly. See how it blurs your perception of broader realities. And notice how it contracts your attention into an attitude of intense self-involvement.

Observe how, by self-involvement, you become impris-
oned in littleness. At the same time, remember to remain an
observer, detached from ego-involvement, lest self-justification
only reveal its reverse side: self-loathing and self-blame.

Once you see that emotion clearly with all its ramifica-
tions, you will find it easier to release it. In the release, offer it
up to inner soul-freedom, at the point between the eyebrows.

.   •   •   •   •   •

Visualization

Continue the visualization of the earlier chapters.

Standing on the river bank, visualize your center in
your own heart. The flowing ripples of consciousness can be
calmed by love. Send out a blessing, as I suggested earlier in
this chapter, from your heart to all the world.

As you do so, notice how the river current changes its
appearance. The surface is no longer agitated by countless ripples. It is becoming peaceful. Behold in the calm water, now,
the reflection of the "promised Eden" beyond it. Reach out
mentally with great longing toward that paradise.

CHAPTER SIX

❋

Concentration

It is time to consider in greater depth the significance of concentrating at the point between the eyebrows.

This point is known as the Christ center, or, in Sanskrit, as *Kutastha Chaitanya*. It is here that the meditator, when deeply concentrated, beholds the spiritual eye or third eye, a phenomenon that has been known since ancient times.

Legends thousands of years old describe this third eye as being situated in the center of the forehead. Artists have depicted it as a half moon. Modern scholars dismiss the entire concept as fanciful, or as merely symbolic. But then, few scholars know much about meditative practices; the under-standing they admire is intellectual. It has been interesting to me over the years, when I've described the spiritual eye to people who were new to meditation, to hear some of them exclaim, "Oh, so *that's* what I've seen!" The spiritual eye may have appeared to them during early attempts to calm their minds, or even as they were on the point of falling asleep.

The spiritual eye is a reflection of the astral[*] light in the medulla oblongata. The Christ center, where it resides, repre-sents the positive pole of the medulla which is, as I said earlier, the seat of ego-consciousness. When this light is beheld perfectly, it takes the form of a five-pointed star set in a field of deep blue or violet light, and circled by a shining ring of gold. In a state of ecstasy, the consciousness penetrates the spiritual eye and enters the inner realms. Truly, as Jesus Christ put it, "The kingdom of God *is* within."

The consciousness of most human beings is centered in the medulla oblongata. Everything they do, think, and per-ceive, being centered in ego-awareness, originates from this point of awareness.

[*]   The astral world is a subtle realm of energy that lies behind this material universe, creating and defining it. For a fuller description, you might refer to chapter 31 of Yogananda's book *The Rubaiyat of Omar Khayyam Explained* (Crystal Clarity Publishers).

The consciousness of enlightened beings, on the other hand, is centered in the Christ center between the eyebrows. All their actions, thoughts, and perceptions originate from that point.

It is good to deepen your awareness of the medulla, since it is the point through which consciousness and energy must pass in order to reach the Christ center. The goal, however, is to reach the Christ center. To remain blocked in the medulla would be to feed ego-consciousness. (Notice, in this context, the way proud people tend to hold and move their heads.)

In meditation, concentrate at a point midway between the eyebrows. Raise your gaze upward—not crossing the eyes, but focusing them on a point somewhat beyond the forehead at about the distance of your thumb when you hold your arm extended above you. Don't be too exact in this matter, however. The important thing is that your *attention* be focused at the point between the eyebrows.

Remember those signs that one used to see at rural railroad crossings? "Stop! Look! Listen!" That is what you should do now:

Stop worrying and planning. The world will still be there when you come out of meditation. Leave things, for this brief period, to their own devices.

Don't *look*, merely: Gaze deeply into, and *behind,* the darkness you behold at the point between the eyebrows when your eyes are closed. The more intently you gaze, with deep calmness, the sooner you will behold at the center of that darkness an island-like area of blue or violet light, surrounded, perhaps, by a faint circle of white. The light may be dim at first, but it will present the beginning of what will take shape, in time, as the spiritual eye.

Listen!—not with the ear only, but with your entire being. Feel yourself in sympathetic resonance with the vibrations of inner silence.

The ancient Greeks, who were in closer contact with the Eastern teachings than people generally realize, referred to the "music of the spheres." This was a poetic description of a phenomenon that was treated at length by the sages of ancient India: a sound that emanates from the heart of creation, bringing consciousness into outer manifestation, maintaining it, and dissolving it back again, finally, into the Infinite Spirit. This sound is the "Word" of the New Testament. It is the "Amen" of the Book of Revelation. In India, this cosmic sound was given the name AUM.

Listen intently in the right ear, especially, to any subtle sound you hear. It is not likely that you will hear AUM clearly at first, but concentration on any internal sound will help you gradually to attune your consciousness to the subtle Cosmic Vibration.

The spiritual sounds are usually heard in the right ear, not in the left. If you hear them in the left ear, try to bring that perception gradually to the right ear. Unite your perception of them with the stillness at the Christ center. Surrender your mind, heart, and body to the Infinite Vibration.

The point between the eyebrows is the seat of concentration in the body. Notice how, whenever you concentrate deeply, you have a tendency to knit your eyebrows. Notice also how you tend to look upward. People with powerful concentration will often have one or two deep furrows in their foreheads between the eyebrows.

The Christ center is also the seat of superconscious ecstasy. Notice also how, whenever you feel particularly happy, you have a tendency to look upward—even, perhaps, to lift your eyebrows.

You may have read about "body language." The body has been found to reveal our mental states. Physical movements and postures are manifestations of the flow of life-force, which in turn responds to our thoughts and feelings.

When we feel depressed, our life-force flows downward in the spine and, sympathetically, in the whole body. When we feel elated, the life-force flows upward.

When your energy flows downward, don't you notice a tendency to lower your head? to look downward? to lower the corners of your mouth, let your shoulders sag and your spine slump? When you stand, perhaps you've noticed that you rest your weight heavily on the heels. Your very gait is heavy.

When the energy flows upward, on the other hand, your posture changes. You raise your head. You look upward. Your mouth curves up in a smile. You sit up straight. When standing, your weight rests on the balls of your feet. When walking, you do so with a light step.

Look upward now in meditation. Send the life-force in your body flowing upward. Release it from your ego-center in the medulla, as if to free it from its earthliness. Send it forward and out through the Christ center. You are an eagle, soaring on powerful wing beats of divine aspiration.

Remember those rays of energy that I suggested you visualize flowing out from your heart center? Think of your heart, now, as a water lily. (In Eastern tradition that lily would be a lotus.) See the lily's petals spread out in all directions, as they do when lying on the surface of a pond. Think of those heart-petals as rays of light and energy flowing out to interact with the world.

Now, mentally turn those petals, those rays of light and energy, upward. They no longer seek to interact with the world, but reach upward in love and aspiration toward the Divine. Visualize your heart's feelings rising in devotion toward the Supreme Being, whose altar is in the brain at the Christ center. There, in the spiritual eye, stands the gateway to Infinity.

Offer yourself upward in deep stillness to the very highest that is in you.

•   •   •   •   •

Questions and Answers

Question: *Since the seat of concentration is at the point between the eyebrows, would it be helpful to knit the eyebrows gently while meditating?*

Answer: Sometimes, perhaps, not as a continuous practice. Don't meditate with your body. Try to release your mind from body-consciousness.

Question: *Would it be good for me to keep my consciousness centered at the point between the eyebrows even when I'm not meditating, and during daily activity?*

Answer: It would be indeed. Yogananda stated that spiritual progress can be greatly accelerated by keeping one's mind focused all the time at the Christ center.

Question: *Can you suggest a way of keeping the mind focused there? I do so many things during the day, and must think about them as well. My thoughts get pulled away from the inwardness I feel when I meditate.*

Answer: Well, it isn't easy to be inward, particularly nowadays, with the many demands placed upon us. There are certain aspects of modern life, however, that can be turned to excellent—even to unprecedented—advantage.

Television and computer screens, for example, and the even newer technology known as "virtual reality," suggest an altogether new approach to keeping the mind inwardly focused.

One problem with visualizing the Christ center during activity is that it represents mental fixity. Everything we do outwardly, however, involves motion. It is difficult enough even while meditating to bring the mind to a still focus. During activity, this difficulty is increased a thousandfold.

Here, then, is a suggestion: Visualize a video screen at the point between the eyebrows! Project your mind through the screen, as if through a window, into a world of "virtual reality." That is in fact what everything around us is: a world of *virtual* reality. It is an illusion, simply—more real to us than any video we see only because it is faithful to all five of the senses, and not only to the senses of hearing and sight. Nevertheless, it is not more real, fundamentally, than any video movie.

As you act and interact with the world around you, and with others, project your consciousness and energy out to them through the "video screen" of your spiritual eye!

•   •   •   •   •

Visualization

It is important in meditation to develop concentration. The following visualization will help you to focus your mind.

Stand mentally on the river bank, where you waited at the end of the last chapter, prevented from crossing the river by the turbulent flow of your own thoughts and feelings. Visualize yourself, now, holding a string that is attached to a balloon filled with helium. The balloon tugs at your hand as it tries to free itself and rise into the sky.

Now, release the string. Watch the balloon as it soars up into the sky, steadily becoming smaller and smaller in the distance. Watch it intently. Let all your thoughts converge on that single object. Slowly it diminishes in size as it rises above the clouds.

A breeze is carrying it toward the far-off mountains. Now the balloon rises above the mountains. As it grows steadily smaller, it disappears at last into the empty sky.

CHAPTER SEVEN

❄

How Long Should One Meditate?

Spiritual practices have been identified for centuries with ego-active concepts, such as acquiring merit, working off bad karma, and propitiating God. Holiness has been gauged by the amount of time a person spends in prayer and meditation, or by the number of beads he tells and *mantras* he utters, or by whether he has suffered—or, according to certain schools of thought, not suffered.

There is nothing wrong with the idea that you get good karma for performing actions. Nor is there anything wrong with wanting to please God. Quite the contrary. It is well also to remember, however, that good karma alone will not get you God, who is beyond all karma. God, moreover, is *always* pleased! He lives in eternal bliss. It is absurd to think of Him (or Her) as an angry Deity waiting gloatingly for the chance to vent His (or Her) displeasure on poor, perennially confused humanity.

Religious teachings, if they are true, are divine. Many religious *beliefs*, however, are little better than superstitions. In the case of judgment, it is people who judge themselves through their uneasy conscience when they offend against higher laws of their own nature. God loves them no matter what they do. His love is infinitely greater than ours for our own children. Even if our child errs, the sorrow we feel, if our love is pure, will be for them and not for ourselves. Our lament will be for the potential they've neglected for true happiness and understanding.

Soul-freedom, however, is not attained by good deeds alone. Spiritual progress is not a matter of winning brownie points. Even though tests are a part of the spiritual path—as they are of life generally—spirituality is determined by the wisdom we acquire as a result of those trials, and not by the trials themselves. The *way out* of our trials is by calm acceptance and a spirit of inner joy. We demonstrate no inner gains if we allow those trials to pull us down into ego-consciousness, with its attendant sorrows.

Keep this thought, therefore, firmly in mind: The way to advance through meditation is not grimly to force yourself to sit as many hours as possible every day. To meditate to the point of mental exhaustion is counter-productive. Don't *push* yourself beyond your own natural abilities. To meditate five minutes may sometimes be more effective than to meditate hours, if during those five minutes you meditate with full concentration and heart-felt dedication. Always try to meditate with enthusiasm—calm, never restless.

In the beginning you may not derive much actual joy from meditating, though you should at least be able to feel peace. In any case, concentrate on the positive results you anticipate from meditation, and not on the arduousness of the effort involved. Later, as you begin to experience joy within, make it a practice to meditate only as long as that joy lasts. When it begins to diminish, stop, and get up. An act that is happily remembered will be returned to with enthusiasm. Never let your meditations become a chore for you.

On the other hand, we've all experienced times when peace, though it is something we long for, seems to be the one thing we most fear. During periods of emotional tension, we may imagine that the only way to rid ourselves of that tension will be to increase it to a fever pitch until it falls away, like an over-ripe fruit, of its own weight.

Truly, every state of mind is a vortex: It sucks into itself any energy that is available to it.

When the mind resists your efforts to calm it, don't squelch its rebellion. Let your thoughts strut for a while. Meanwhile, simply watch them—pleasantly, if you can, even good-humoredly, as you might watch a fractious child. They will calm down once they find that you respect them no less for their unruliness. During periods of restlessness, when the mind is concerned with busily declaring its independence, don't discipline it too sternly. Meditate some, of course, if only to keep the meditative habit alive, but otherwise divert the mind. Don't punish yourself for your inadequacies.

A good rule in meditation generally is to *keep always relaxed*. Don't "tough it out" when you feel restless. Instead, work at *loving God more deeply*.

It isn't easy to formulate a single rule that will fit everybody's needs. There are many gradations of spiritual commitment. The person who longs intensely for God may want to devote every waking moment to his spiritual life. For another person, even one hour a day may seem exaggerated. The "path of moderation," so often recommended by great masters, is always meant to signify that one shouldn't strain. Balanced progress demands ever deeper relaxation. On the other hand, a sincere seeker will always devote much time to meditation. It is only by worldly minds that "moderation" is taken to mean, "Be as restless as you like, as long as you spend a little time also in meditation."

Whatever your own definition of moderation, try to make daily meditation a pleasure, not a chore. Start, if you like, with five minutes a day. Don't worry if others, beginners like yourself, sit for half an hour or even an hour. It is always risky to compare yourself with others. Find your own natural rhythms. First of all, get accustomed simply to sitting still for a while; it is better to meditate a little bit than not at all. A better length for beginners, however, would be fifteen minutes—enough time, in other words, to give the mind an opportunity to "simmer down" a little.

Gradually, after a few days or weeks, see if you can't double your meditation time. Then double it again. Once you begin really to enjoy meditating, you'll find it natural to sit longer.

Ideally, I'd suggest meditating twice a day, half an hour at each sitting. Don't force yourself, but try to reach the point where you realize that what you are doing is important to you. From then on, you'll be safely on your own! At that point, I would say to meditate at least an hour and a half a day—an hour, perhaps, in the morning, and half an hour in the evening. At Ananda Village, and in the branch Ananda communities, I recommend that our members try to meditate a minimum of three hours a day.

Apart from these few guidelines, the matter is up to you. What seems "moderation" to one may strike another as fanatical excess. And what seems "moderation" to that other may strike the first as a sure indication of tepidity.

Above all, be steadfast. It is better to meditate regularly for a few minutes every day than to make heroic efforts for a week, and then, one's will power exhausted, collapse into a state of spiritual paralysis.

Remember, finally, this simple rule; it was stated by Paramhansa Yogananda: "The more you meditate, the more you'll want to meditate. But the less you meditate, the less you'll want to meditate."

• • • • •

Questions and Answers

Question: *Why is my mind so resistant? I find sometimes that my very resolution to do better is enough to inspire an in-house rebellion!*

Answer: Habit can be a potent adversary, as I've pointed out before. The good thing is that habit can also become a powerful ally. Develop the right habits and they'll pull you safely through many a fierce storm.

It takes time, usually, to uproot bad habits—even as much time as five to eight years, in the case of deeply rooted ones. The way to uproot them is not so much by fighting them as by working all the harder at developing opposite good habits.

Restlessness, for example, is overcome by developing a taste for calmness. A tendency to talk excessively can be overcome by developing a liking for silence. Paramhansa Yogananda used to say, "You can't get rid of darkness by beating at it with a stick. Instead, turn on the light! The darkness will then vanish as though it had never been."

Question: *You raised the subject of opposition from outer circumstances. What can I do if family members, friends, or co-workers try to keep me from meditating?*

Answer: This kind of opposition often comes in reaction to proselytizing efforts on the new meditator's part. It is better, in the beginning especially, to keep your spiritual practices to yourself, or to share them only with those whom you know to be sympathetic. As Yogananda put it, "If you pour milk on water, it will mingle with the water. But once the milk has been churned to butter, it will float naturally and not become diluted."

No one will protest if you spend more time than most people in brushing your teeth. If you sleep longer than necessary, those closest to you may not like it, but most people will simply think it might be better if you didn't. They'd actively oppose you only if you insisted that everyone do likewise.

Keep your spiritual practices to yourself. They are no one's business but your own.

Question: *Another thought arises with the suggestion of outside opposition. In reading the lives of saints, it seems they were often subjected to satanic influences. Do such influences really exist? And if so, ought we to be concerned about them in our spiritual life?*

Answer: A satanic influence, so called, is anything that obstructs your efforts toward self-improvement. It could be a hostile co-worker who thrives on disharmony, and can't stand to see you peaceful. The negative influence, in other words, needn't be an imp with a tail! But one would have to be blind not to see that obstructive influences do exist in our lives.

So then, could more be involved in such opposition than the resistance of other people to your spiritual efforts? Is there a negative force that can pursue you even past the door that you close to ensure meditative privacy?

Well, there are of course your own thoughts. What door could shut them out?

But is there also something else—a malign influence, perhaps on a cosmic scale?

It wouldn't hurt to be aware that human thoughts are expressions of states of consciousness that are universal. For instance, we don't *create* love: We *manifest* it. We don't *create* inspiration: We *receive* it. The same must be said of negative thoughts and emotions. We attract the states of consciousness that come to us.

As for being concerned about such negative influences, don't invite them by your excessive anxiety. I think that much of the "satanic" influence that people experience comes in response to their own preoccupation with the subject. Be positive. *Reach upward* in your aspirations, not downward in your fears. If negative thoughts enter the mind, don't accept them. The thoughts are not yours, and don't define you as you are. They are foreigners, no matter how many years you've housed and fed them in your mind. Tell yourself, "I am a child of God. From now on I define myself in terms of my strengths, not of my past weaknesses."

Question: *You've discussed how long to meditate on a daily basis. How long will it take me to reach the goals of meditation—to attain superconscious awareness, for instance, or to find God?*

Answer: The time varies with the individual, of course. If a nail is partly embedded in a board, can you say how long it will take to extract it? It depends on the length of the embedded portion, on how tightly set it is, and on the amount of force you apply to pull the nail.

How long, then, does it take to achieve the goals of meditation? It depends on the number and fixity of the bad habits that are buried in the subconscious, which work against your present meditative efforts. It depends on how fervently you apply yourself.

Finally, it depends on the grace of God. But grace is not whimsical. It is poured into that bowl which has been made clean. "Blessed are the pure in heart," Jesus said, "for they shall know God."

There is another important point to consider: Time, in the last analysis, is a delusion. If the spiritual path requires time, it is partly because of our belief, born of past conditioning, that time is a reality to be reckoned with. Yet the truth we seek lies beyond time, in eternity. If we could only banish the delusion of time from our minds, our spiritual journey might be ended even now! The path is a process of realizing—of *remembering*—that which we are already. Our soul's perfection can never be lost. We have hypnotized ourselves, merely, with the thought of limitation. We have told ourselves, falsely, that our limitations define us as we are.

•   •   •   •   •

Visualization

Stand again on the near side of the river bank, as you've done before. The time has now come for you to cross the river.

How will you do so?

You may use one of the methods I've suggested already: Wait for the river to subside, until its bed is dry—or, if you prefer, divide the waters by your will power and cross over between the separated walls.

Today, though, a third method suggests itself: Project love to your restless thoughts and feelings. Calm the turbulence of the flowing water, and see reflected in its still surface the land of mystic beauty beyond them.

Time is a delusion. If you think yourself on the other side of the river, it will be so. If you think yourself at the foot of those distant mountains, this, too, will be so.

Be there now!

On the crest of a low foothill of the mountains you find a large balloon, straining upward above its basket. It has been waiting for you. The guylines tying the basket to the ground represent certain remaining attachments to the world. Climb into the basket and untie those lines one by one, releasing them. You may also, if you prefer, sever the lines vigorously with a large knife.

See—the balloon is starting to rise. Feel that the helium which lifts it is the soaring power of your devotion: The more intense your heart's aspiration, the more rapid will be your ascent.

Do you see? There was no need to scale those high mountains laboriously. You are rising much faster, and far higher, by the simple power of love!

As you rise, you attain altitudes from time to time above which the balloon won't rise any higher. Each time this happens, empty one of the sandbags that hang from the edge of your basket. The grains of sand are small, lingering attachments in your heart. Scatter them joyfully into the air. Rejoice as the balloon once again resumes its upward climb.

The last sandbag has now been emptied. Lo! You are free!

CHAPTER EIGHT

❋

After Meditation

Learn to live more *superconsciously*. This means to live with meditation-born awareness. Try to make the peace you experience in meditation the basis of your objective experience of life. Don't let the meditative peace slip between your fingers like grains of sand the moment you find the winds of worldly duties again buffeting you.

Don't let the insistent demands people make of you blow away your calm self-awareness.

Don't let others define you in their terms. Live by what you know of yourself, inwardly. Your abiding reality is the peace, love, and joy you have experienced in your own soul.

Meditation makes you aware of a better world. It is no dream world, but a world more real than any other. Owing to your awareness of that world, you will be able to cope far more effectively with things and situations that others around you insist are the world of reality. Peace will help you to solve problems that others, living as they are, hemmed in by cares and worries, find insoluble.

Calmness will come to you as a result of daily meditation. In that calmness will come intuitive perceptions. Where, formerly, you may have felt paralyzed by the sheer enormity of life's *problems*, intuition will supply you with simple, clear *answers*.

You will find through meditation a heart quality developing that will inspire others to look at their problems, too, more constructively.

Meditation will sharpen your concentration, and develop your will power. Obstacles of many kinds will simply vanish, and you'll be able to accomplish in minutes what, formerly, might have taken you hours, days, or even weeks to do.

A highly successful businessman of my acquaintance spent his mornings meditating. He went to work only in the afternoons. His associates sometimes chided him, "With all your responsibilities, how can you afford to be so late for work?"

"Because of my responsibilities," he would reply, "I can't afford not to!" He had found that by coming to work with a clear mind he could solve problems on which others would have spent days, without ever being sure whether the answers they found were the right ones.

For intuition, the natural fruit of meditation, has one supreme advantage over the reasoning faculty: It provides inner certainty.

The rational mind can never be quite sure of anything. The best it ever does is decide on which, out of a variety of possibilities, seems the best choice. Great discoveries and accomplishments are the consequence, always, of some measure of intuition.

Learn to look at life more with a sense of its underlying unity. Don't analyze everything. Obviously, there are situations where analysis is necessary, but even then, cling to a deeper consciousness of the interrelationship of all things. For everything is a manifestation of a universal reality—even as waves, whatever shape they manifest, are manifestations of the same sea.

There is a coherency in life, an underlying purpose and meaning. *Know* that, for every problem, there *has* to be a solution. See other people, not (to quote Sartre) as "that which you are not," but as part of your own greater reality. Love them from that inward awareness which you are developing in meditation. All humanity is, in the deeper sense, your own self.

All things are subject to the Law of Oneness. Everything has its compensating opposite. The pendulum, after moving in one direction, swings back in the opposite direction. For every up there is a down; for every left, a right; for every negative, a positive. Darkness and light, cold and heat, pain and pleasure, male and female—in all Nature we see opposites balancing one another.

For every problem, similarly, there is a solution. Be solution-oriented, not problem-oriented. That is what it means to think superconsciously. Don't dwell on difficulties longer than it takes simply to define them clearly. The solutions often come from seeing opposites as pairs in a single unity.

Be guided, above all, by inner joy. The more you let yourself be guided superconsciously, the more you will feel joy in everything you do. You will reach the point of understanding that, if that quiet, inner joy is missing, anything you contemplate doing were better left undone. And when inner joy is present, it will be your way of knowing for a certainty that what you contemplate is right and good.

•   •   •   •   •

Questions and Answers

Question: *How can I be* really sure *that I'm being guided superconsciously?*

Answer: You can't be absolutely certain; the mind is very adept at fooling itself! You *can*, however, become increasingly satisfied with the results, as everything you do works increasingly effectively for you.

Don't abandon reason in your attempt to be guided superconsciously. Reason is a valuable tool for understanding. It is the corrector. Though not creative in itself, it is an important part of the creative process. Reason checks your conclusions objectively and helps you to make sure they will really work.

Reason looks at the ideal and sees whether, in application to prosaic reality, the ideal will work.

Nikola Tesla, for example, the great inventor,* "invented" a number of marvels that had to await the discovery of new materials before they could be made practicable. His inspiration outstripped the practical knowledge of his times. Superconscious guidance will be true, but it may be true before its time in this world of prosaic realities. Sometimes, also, guidance comes mixed with human desires and expectations. Reason will help you to separate the true from that which you merely wish to be true.

Question: *How will "solution-orientedness" in itself bring me solutions? I may wish for a solution, but I don't see how, if I'm not really functioning on a superconscious level in a state of deep meditation, mere wishing for answers will supply them to me.*

Answer: What "solution-orientedness" does is open your mind to inspiration "from above" by attuning it to the way that inspiration works. "Solution-orientedness" carries no guarantee, but great inspirations always come by putting out the positive faith, first, that the answers exist, and that they are simply wait-

* Tesla discovered alternating current, which made possible the modern world of electricity.

ing to be found. Have faith that you have them already, and you'll be surprised how often your faith is justified.

Question: *What is the best way to carry my meditation-born awareness into daily life?*

Answer: By developing a consciousness of your own center in the spine. Live outward from that center, rather than inward from your periphery.

• • • • •

Visualization

The balloon beneath which you were ascending in the last visualization is now carrying you high above the mountain peaks. Look down below you at the vast countryside: at the busy city you left behind, at the road as it winds through peaceful meadows, at the tree-dense forest, and at the river twisting its way through the plains. See the foothills rising and meeting the high mountains.

Observe everywhere a unifying reality. Nothing, in itself, is complete. Everything below you is part of a totality which, taken all together, is right, good, and beautiful. The very anxiety and noise of the city were necessary; they provide a comparison, a choice. What, you ask yourself, did your ego want? Did it really *want* bondage, pain, and suffering? Never! You know now what you wanted far more deeply than the immediate goals you sought. You wanted expansive peace, soul-freedom, wisdom!

Rise higher still with your balloon's ascent. There is no feeling of cold about you as the balloon soars into the stratosphere. Nor is there a feeling of warmth. Your body is becoming diminishingly real. Weight no longer exists. There is nothing firm around you. You are becoming space itself— circumscribed vaguely by the balloon, with its increasingly non-material basket.

Higher still you go—into outer space. Behold the round earth spinning slowly beneath you. Realize that it, too, is but a part of your infinitely greater reality—a reality that includes the moon, sun, planets, and all the stars.

Until today you have retained your human center: your little sense of "I." But what is this "I," when there is no one else to relate to, not forests, nor plains, nor mountains to remind you how very little your body was?

Cast away the last of your earthly attachments. Pour
out the little grains of sand, representing your last, lingering
earthly tendencies. Release your ego from its little nest of secu-
rity. Offer yourself into the vastness of space all around you.
Embrace the galaxies. You are they, and so much, much more.

The very universe is *you!*

Rejoice calmly in your newly discovered liberty: in your
freedom from littleness! Dwell on that image of vastness, until
you feel that infinity is what you truly are.

CHAPTER NINE

✳

Meditation as a Daily Guide

There are two reasons why I've named this book *Meditation for Starters*. The first is obvious: It is to help beginners make a start, though I hope that others also, for whom meditation is a regular practice, will find this book helpful.

The second reason is less obvious. My intention is also to encourage you to use meditation as an important *start*, every time you set out to do something. The more you resort to meditation as a daily guide, the more you will find everything you do being crowned with success and with deep, inner satisfaction.

Meditation should become as much a part of your daily pattern of living as eating, talking, and sleeping. Please don't make the mistake of thinking of what I've offered you as an *alternative* to a normal life. Oh, yes, I've offered you an alternative to something you may have *thought* of as "normal"—an existence without any sense of life's ultimate purpose and meaning. I've offered you an alternative to living in confusion, with an endless repetition of purposeless suffering. I've offered you expansive awareness as an alternative to self-preoccupation, joy as an alternative to bitterness and disillusionment, love as an alternative to negative emotions such as hatred, jealousy, and anger.

I guess it comes down to what people consider normal. But, surely, it must be normal for everyone at least to *want* fulfillment in life, and to want happiness. It must be abnormal, then, to deny one's spiritual aspirations.

Don't simply decide in advance that spiritual truths are unattainable. You may never have met anyone who has been to the North Pole: Does that mean no one could ever go there? or that the North Pole doesn't even exist? There are people in this world who give evidence of having attained what they claim to be the *summum bonum* of life. Regardless of that claim, they are people without exception whose company others seek for the peace and happiness they experience in their presence.

A thing is not normal merely because everybody does it. A thing is normal if it can give people what everybody is seeking, even if most of them seek it in mistaken ways.

Meditation may seem exotic at first, particularly if no one you know practices it. The more you do it, however, the more it will assume for you a central role in your life. It will become so deeply meaningful to you that you would no more think of giving it up than you'd think of giving up sleep.

Before every undertaking, then, spend even a short time centering yourself in the inner silence. Focus your attention in the heart, and at the point between the eyebrows. Attune yourself, however briefly and imperfectly, to your own superconscious.

A guitar string sounds loud when it is vigorously plucked, because it produces resonance in the sounding board. Without resonance, the sound would be so thin it might not be heard even across the room. Bring "resonance" to your life from higher levels of reality, by attuning yourself to those levels, inwardly.

Obviously, you can't go into deep meditation every time some issue needs deciding instantly, or some problem needs to be addressed on the spur of the moment. With practice, however, you'll find you can *instantly* recall your center to mind, and radiate energy outward from that center rather than reacting hastily or emotionally to situations confronting you.

You must train your mind gradually. It takes time to establish new habit patterns. The more you work at it, the more you will find meditation bringing a new and fuller sense of meaning to your life. It's really as simple as this: If you insist on living at your periphery, and on ignoring the source of life in yourself, you will find yourself becoming increasingly hollow inside. But once you understand that the secret of life is to live more at your own center, you will find abundant nourishment for everything you do.

My dear friend: May you know ever-new joy!

·   ·   ·   ·   ·

Questions and Answers

Question: *What if my wife, or husband, is opposed to my meditating? I don't want to create disharmony in my married life.*

Answer: It would not be right for anyone to try to deprive you of true happiness and meaning in your life. To do so would introduce far greater disharmony into your relationship, eventually, than anything else possibly could.

Out of regard for your spouse's misunderstanding of what you are doing, and in order not to introduce disharmony by arguing the point, you may simply have to face the fact that married life is not and never can be a perfect fusion of two minds. Each partner must preserve his own integrity, and respect the integrity of the other, even while trying to bring two separate realities into harmony with one another.

There are thoughts that you may not be able to share with one another if—I might even say, *especially* if—you want to maintain harmony between you. Misunderstandings may easily arise, if you are not gentle in the way you phrase your thoughts even about simple matters. Don't worry, then, that you might betray your spouse by keeping your spiritual pursuits to yourself, if there is not the will on the other's part to understand them. The more peaceful you become in yourself, surely, the greater the chances of bringing peace to your marital relationship.

You could meditate after your spouse has gone to sleep. Or you could meditate on your lunch hour—in a local church, perhaps. You could even meditate, however briefly, in the bathroom! "Where there's a will," goes the well-known adage, "there's a way."

Question: *What do you consider the best way for receiving inner guidance?*

Answer: Hold your demand up to the superconscious at the point between the eyebrows, or pray to God at that point. Then "listen" for a responsive feeling in your heart (in the area of the spine, that is to say, opposite the heart). As your intuition develops, you will sense a positive answer there, or, alternately, a negative warning—a feeling of "better not."

If no answer comes, hold up a tentative answer to the Christ center, and ask again, "Is this all right?" A succession of tentative answers may finally produce the response you seek.

Oftentimes, answers will come only after you begin acting according to your best understanding. If no answer comes in meditation, therefore, do what seems sensible to you, but keep inwardly tuned to see if you don't at some point feel the guidance you've been seeking. You will feel it, in time, if you keep on trying.

A final caution: Don't consider *any* guidance to be final. Many times, inner guidance is for this moment only. Keep inwardly tuned to see what further guidance comes, as you proceed.

•   •   •   •   •

Visualization

Your soaring balloon has carried you high into outer space. Your spirit has expanded outward into the solar system, then out into the universe. Meditate again on that vastness. It is YOU!

Realize that there is no emptiness, anywhere. Fill the universe with light and joy. Feel their presence not only throughout space—that is, throughout what seems to us, with our human senses, to be space—but imagine them also scintillating brilliantly from every star, and received in turn—as desert travelers receive water—by every planet.

Light—joy—peace—love: everywhere in the universe, in every atom, in all the atoms of your being!

Imagine the sun now as a spectacularly bright star. Watch, as a ray of its light shoots out and touches a single point on our little planet Earth. Glide down that shaft of light as it descends to earth, and see it come to a focus on your own town, your neighborhood, your very home. Lo! It is entering your body and filling it with light, love, and joy.

Imagine bliss transforming your clothing into light—filling every cell of your body, animating and directing all your thoughts and feelings. Bliss flows *through* you, now, to accomplish even the mundane tasks of your earthly existence.

You are no mere human being: You are a child of Eternal Light. Live constantly in that awareness within.

THE END

PART TWO

❋

Land of Mystery

The companion recording, enclosed in the back of this book, includes 30-minutes of practical instruction in meditation by Swami Kriyananda, followed by 30-minutes of uplifting music with guided imagery titled *Land of Mystery*. Allow the following text to help guide you to your personal Land of Mystery, that inner haven where every thought is in tune with the soothing music of nature.

We would also like to invite you to view our online meditation resources. Just type the link below into your browser.

http://www.ananda.org/meditation/support/index.html

Follow the different links on the left hand navigation bar. Click on the "Meditation for Starters Video" link to see a 25-minute video of Swami Kriyananda discussing how to meditate. Sign-up for the *Daily Meditator* eNewsletter. Read about meditation and follow the links to more resources to help you with your meditation practice.

Please enjoy all the additional meditation resources that we offer throughout the website and feel free to contact us with your questions.

Land of Mystery

�֍

Where do clouds sail,
When they leave the shining sunset behind?
They sail for the Land of Mystery!
Will they find what they seek?
That depends on you!
For the breeze that blows them
Is the breath of your own peace.
Let the clouds sail—
Sail away—
Far, far away:
Over distant horizons,
Over gently rolling hills,
Over deserts, where tiny, slow-moving caravans

Wind their way patiently toward waiting oases.
Sail with the clouds above the vast oceans,
Their heaving swells rising, sinking, constantly,
As if slowly breathing.
Sail above wide prairies,
Soaring, snow-clad mountains,
Dense forests,
And sleepy towns with lamplit, winding streets
Guarded by tall, watchful clock towers.
Sail over farmlands—little, patchwork quilts
Of green, gold, and walnut-brown.
Fly far, ever farther—
Until at last you come
To a land of golden light.
A long way below you,
White beaches, washed by soothing waves,
Call to you, "Come to us:
Sleep on our soft sands!"
A deep blue sea murmurs through the rolling surf:
"Rest and listen, while I sing to you."
And palm trees, rustling in the breeze,
Draw your gaze inland,

Where emerald-green hills call to you invitingly:
"Play here in our golden sunshine!"
Why not go there?
Leave the great, sailing clouds
For this Land of Mystery.
Sky-dive—freely down gentle breezes,
Gliding, swooping, soaring,
Then at last slowly sinking,
To land gently in a forest glade.
Walk on the green, mossy floor,
Its touch cool on your bare feet.
Long shafts of sunlight slant downward,
Like stairways from the sky.
The forest you've entered is a friendly one.
Fawns gambol nearby you, or graze quietly;
Gaily colored birds flit from tree to tree
Through the slanting sun rays,
And tame, kindly animals
Pause from time to time to gaze at you
And nod in friendly fashion.
As you wander down leaf-bordered aisles
You say to yourself,

"How beautiful it all is!—
But what makes this a Land of *Mystery*?
Is beauty mysterious?
Is friendliness?"
And just then, walking happily,
You smile.
Ah, look!
Aren't the shafts of sunlight through the trees
A little brighter?
Call to a deer: It glances up,
Then comes over and nuzzles you.
Stretch out your hand to a bird, and,
In a lively swirl of red and blue,
It swoops down to land on your forefinger.
A dainty pink-and-white blossom
High above your head makes you think,
"I wish I could hold you!
If only I could enjoy your fragrance!"
And just then, the long, thin branch reaches down
And lets you smell the blossom.
Now do you understand?
This land is mysterious because

It reflects your thoughts!
Why (you ask)?
Because you and it are in harmony.
Then, again—*Why?*
Because your heart is at peace.
How wonderfully uplifting, this harmony!
Embrace it!
As you do so,
A cresting wave of joy breaks over you,
And a chord of angelic music
Pours through the trees in a stream of radiant light.
Rise in the air, effortlessly, with that glorious sound.
On streams of music soar down quiet glades,
Above grassy knolls,
And over flower-scattered thickets;
Up shafts of sunlight, then down again,
Soaring and swooping like a bird.
After some time, come again to earth
In an open field at the edge of the forest.
On a bush of yellow blossoms
Sits a blue butterfly, brilliant in the sunlight.
Spying you, it flutters over,

And hovers on a level with your eyes.
"Follow me," whispers the butterfly,
Then flits lightly away, leading you.
Soon you emerge onto an emerald meadow.
Wildflowers of countless, laughing colors
Wink at you merrily through the long grass
That sways gently in the breeze.
Laugh and skip in the meadow,
Playing with the butterfly!
Then sit quietly
And breathe the sweet scent of the flowers.
Listen!
Can you hear rippling music,
Harp-like on the breeze?
The strings of the harp are the long meadow grass!
Again, now, the butterfly whispers, "Follow me!"
It leads you over low hills,
Through grassy, fragrant meadows,
And beside a gay crystal stream,
Its waters chuckling at the memory
Of some mountain-told, happy story.
At last you see before you the rustling palm trees,

And, beyond them, a wide, sparkling beach,
Spreading a welcome to you of warm sand.
Walk there; listen to the rolling surf:
The waves bring you a message from the sea.
"You are more," they say—
"*so much* more than you know!"
As each wave crests, then curls inward upon itself
To break into a riot of white foam,
It calls to you, "Break your littleness!
You are *so much* more than you realize!"
As the foam flows up onto the beach,
Its soft fingers touch you.
"Won't you listen?" the foam whispers;
Then, withdrawing, it murmurs,
"Rest now: Relax.
Perhaps, then, you'll understand."
Lie back peacefully on the soft sand,
And—quietly—let your mind soar....
Time passes in deep peacefulness.
Now, the blue sea sends another messenger:
A very large, loving wave surges up onto the beach,
And wraps you in a shining tunnel of blue light.

Lose yourself in that light.
Do you hear?
A deep, rolling, rumble
Speaks to you from inside the wave:
"We are one!
Leave your little body, friend—
We are one!"
Melt into the curling wave—
Into the blue light—
Into the vast sea!
Coral castles underwater, orange and red,
Stand sentinel in a dim, luminous world.
Tropical fish of many colors dart about—
In, out, and over tall turrets
And stern battlements—
Flashes of turquoise, brilliant yellow,
Flaming violet, rose—
Courtiers and elegant ladies-in-waiting they seem,
Proud of their rich costumes,
Bustling in service to their king and queen.
Below them, long ferns—like royal flags—
Wave in the shifting currents, reminding you

Of willows swaying in a gentle breeze.
The sun's rays in this underwater kingdom
Form tall columns fading into the distance:
Like shining pillars in a formal garden
Where mist hides the surrounding countryside,
And fairyland terraces are stepped gracefully downward
To a dark, invisible valley.
Gaze into the vanishing unknown.
"We are one!" rumbles the sea.
Your thoughts, your heart's feelings
Expand outward in all directions
To embrace that oneness.
Everything around you is a part of some greater *You:*
Coral castles, terraced hills, dark valleys,
And the vastness of water everywhere—
All this is *You!*
You, a tiny ripple of peace,
Have become, now,
The vast sea of Happiness and Joy!

About the Author

❄

SWAMI KRIYANANDA

"Swami Kriyananda is a man of wisdom and compassion in action, truly one of the leading lights in the spiritual world today."
—Lama Surya Das, Dzogchen Center, author of
Awakening The Buddha Within

A prolific author, accomplished composer, playwright, and artist, and a world-renowned spiritual teacher, Swami Kriyananda refers to himself simply as "a humble disciple" of the great God-realized master, Paramhansa Yogananda. He met his guru at the young age of twenty-two, and served him during the last four years of the Master's life. And he has done so continuously ever since.

During a period of intense inward reflection, he discovered Yogananda's *Autobiography of a Yogi*, and immediately traveled 3,000 miles from New York to California to meet the Master, who accepted him as a monastic disciple. Yogananda appointed him as the head of the monastery, authorized him to teach in his name and to give initiation into Kriya Yoga, and entrusted him with the missions of writing and developing what he called "world-brotherhood colonies." Recognized as the "father of the spiritual communities movement" in the United States, Swami Kriyananda founded Ananda World-Brotherhood Community in 1968. It has served as a model for a number of communities founded subsequently in the United States and Europe.

Further Explorations

❋

If you are inspired by *Meditation for Starters* and would like to learn more about Swami Kriyananda or Paramhansa Yogananda and his teachings, Crystal Clarity Publishers offers many additional resources to assist you.

•   •   •   •   •

If you would like to further your meditation practice or learn how to begin your own practice of yoga postures, Kriya Yoga, and more, as taught by Yogananda and Kriyananda, we recommend the following:

Awaken to Superconsciousness

Meditation for Inner Peace, Intuitive Guidance, and Greater Awareness

Swami Kriyananda

This popular guide includes everything you need to know about the philosophy and practice of meditation, and how to apply the meditative mind to resolving common daily conflicts in uncommon, superconscious ways. Superconsciousness is the hidden mechanism at work behind intuition, spiritual and physical healing, successful problem solving, and finding deep, and lasting, joy.

Praise for Awaken to Superconsciousness

"A brilliant, thoroughly enjoyable guide to the art and science of meditation. [Swami Kriyananda] entertains, informs, and inspires—his enthusiasm for the subject is contagious. This book is a joy to read from beginning to end."

—*Yoga International*

The Art and Science of Raja Yoga

Swami Kriyananda

Contains fourteen lessons in which the original yoga science emerges in all its glory—a proven system for realizing one's spiritual destiny. This is the most comprehensive course available on yoga and meditation today. Over 450 pages of text and photos give you a complete and detailed presentation of yoga postures, yoga philosophy, affirmations, meditation instruction, and breathing techniques. Also included are suggestions for daily yoga routines, information on proper diet, recipes, and alternative healing techniques. The book also comes with an audio CD that contains: a guided yoga postures sessions, a guided meditation, and an inspiring talk on how you can use these techniques to solve many of the problems of daily life.

Praise for The Art and Science of Raja Yoga

"[Kriyananda's] long teaching record shows his ability to discuss key yogic concepts and practices in simple terms. . . . This comprehensive guide has an extra medium to distinguish it on the crowded yoga bookshelf: an accompanying audio CD that contains a vague lecture as well as more helpful sections of guided meditation and posture instruction. All things considered, it's superior to books that reduce yoga to a series of physical exercises taught by this year's guru."

—Publishers Weekly

Affirmations for Self-Healing
Swami Kriyananda

This inspirational book contains 52 affirmations and prayers, each pair devoted to improving a quality in ourselves. Strengthen your will power; cultivate forgiveness, patience, health, and enthusiasm. A powerful tool for self-transformation.

•　•　•　•　•

Crystal Clarity publishes the original, unedited edition of Paramhansa Yogananda's spiritual masterpiece:

Autobiography of a Yogi
Paramhansa Yogananda

This is a new edition, featuring previously unavailable material, of a true spiritual classic, *Autobiography of a Yogi*: one of the best-selling Eastern philosophy titles of all-time, with millions of copies sold, named one of the best and most influential books of the 20th Century.

This highly prized verbatim reprinting of the original 1946 edition is the ONLY one available free from textual changes made after Yogananda's death.

This updated edition contains bonus materials, including a last chapter that Yogananda himself wrote in 1951, five years after the publication of the first edition. It is the only version of this chapter available without posthumous changes.

Yogananda was the first yoga master of India whose mission it was to live and teach in the West. His first-hand account of his life experiences includes childhood revelations, stories of his visits to saints and masters in India, and long-secret teachings of Self-realization that he made available to the Western reader.

Praise for Autobiography of a Yogi
"In the original edition, published during Yogananda's life, one is more in contact with Yogananda himself. While Yogananda founded centers and organizations, his concern was more with guiding individuals

to direct communion with Divinity rather than with promoting any one church as opposed to another. This spirit is easier to grasp in the original edition of this great spiritual and yogic classic."
—Dr. David Frawley, Director, American Institute of Vedic Studies

•　　•　　•　　•　　•

Autobiography of a Yogi is one of the best-selling spiritual biographies of all time. The book is not merely read—it is treasured and cherished by millions of spiritual seekers throughout the world. Now, for the first time, Paramhansa Yogananda's thrilling autobiography comes to new life in this beautiful full-color card deck and booklet.

Autobiography of a Yogi: 52-Cards & Booklet
Paramhansa Yogananda

Each of the 52 cards features an inspiring quotation taken from the text of the Original 1946 First Edition—the preferred edition for both enthusiasts and collectors. The flip-side of each card features a photograph from the book, including previously unreleased and rare photographs of Yogananda. For the first time, these famous images and quotations will be portable, ensuring their use by the great Master's followers in their homes, altars, journals, autos, and purses. The enclosed booklet includes a history of the book, additional information about the quotations and photographs, and includes a user's guide for the cards.

The *Autobiography of a Yogi* is also available in audiobook format. It is the original 1946 edition unabridged, read by one of Yogananda's direct disciples Swami Kriyananda.

•   •   •   •   •

The Wisdom of Yogananda series features writings of Paramhansa Yogananda not available elsewhere. These books capture the Master's expansive and compassionate wisdom, his sense of fun, and his practical spiritual guidance. The books include writings from his earliest years in America, in an approachable, easy-to-read format. The words of the Master are presented with minimal editing, to capture the fresh and original voice of one of the most highly regarded spiritual teachers of the 20th Century.

How to Be Happy All the Time
The Wisdom of Yogananda Series, Volume 1
Paramhansa Yogananda

The human drive for happiness is one of our most far-reaching and fundamental needs. Yet, despite our desperate search for happiness, according to a recent Gallup Poll, only a minority of North Americans describe themselves as "very happy." It seems that very few of us have truly unlocked the secrets of lasting joy and inner peace.

In this volume of all-new, never-before-released material, Paramhansa Yogananda playfully and powerfully explains virtually everything needed to lead a happier, more fulfilling life. Topics covered include: looking for happiness in the right places; choosing to be happy; tools and techniques for achieving happiness; sharing happiness with others; balancing success and happiness, and many more.

Karma and Reincarnation
The Wisdom of Yogananda Series, Volume 2
Paramhansa Yogananda

The interrelated ideas of karma and reincarnation have intrigued us for millennia. In today's post-modern culture, the idea of "karma" has become mainstream while belief in reincarnation is now at an all-time high in the West. Yet, for all of the burgeoning interest, very few of us truly understand what these terms mean and how they work.

In this volume of all-new material, Yogananda definitively reveals the truth behind karma, death, reincarnation, and the afterlife. With clarity and simplicity, Yogananda makes the mysterious understandable. Topics covered include: how karma works; how we can change our karma; the relationship between karma and reincarnation; what we can learn from our past lives; how to overcome karmic obstacles; how to die with uplifted consciousness; what happens after death; the true purpose of life, and much more.

Spiritual Relationships
The Wisdom of Yogananda Series, Volume 3
Paramhansa Yogananda

Discover how to express your own highest potential in relationships of friendship, love, marriage, and family. Warmly, realistically, with humor and humanity, Yogananda shows you the folly of selfishness and the practical steps toward expansive love for others. Learn to experience more harmony in your life. Friendship, love, marriage, and children can offer us our greatest joys in life or our greatest sorrows. Selfless love is the essential key to happiness in all our relationships, but how do we practice it?

In this book Yogananda shares fresh inspiration and practical guidance on: friendship: broadening your sympathies and expanding the boundaries of your love; How to cure bad habits that spell the death of true friendship: judgment, jealousy, over-sensitivity, unkindness, and more; how to choose the right partner and create a lasting marriage; sex in marriage and how to conceive a spiritual child; problems that arise in marriage and what to do about them; the divine plan uniting parents and children; the Universal Love behind all your relationships.

How to Be a Success

The Wisdom of Yogananda Series, Volume 4
Paramhansa Yogananda

Is there a power that can reveal hidden veins of riches and uncover treasures of which we never dreamed? Is there a force that we can call upon to give success, health, happiness, and spiritual enlightenment? The saints and sages of India taught that there is such a power.

Now, in this volume of all-new, never-before-released material, Paramhansa Yogananda—who has millions of followers around the world—shares how we can achieve the highest success of material and spiritual efficiency.

•   •   •   •   •

Yogananda has many direct disciples, individuals that he personally trained to carry on various aspects of his mission after his passing. One of the best known of these disciples is Swami Kriyananda, the founder of Ananda and Crystal Clarity Publishers. Kriyananda's autobiography, a sequel of sorts to *Autobiography of a Yogi*, contains hundreds of stories about Yogananda, culled from the nearly four years that Kriyananda lived with and was trained by Yogananda. It offers the unique perspective of a disciple reflecting on his time with a great Master.

The Path—My Life with Paramhansa Yogananda
One Man's Search on the Only Path there Is
Swami Kriyananda (J. Donald Walters)

The Path is the moving story of Kriyananda's years with Paramhansa Yogananda. *The Path* completes Yogananda's life story and includes more than 400 never-before-published stories about Yogananda, India's emissary to the West and the first yoga master to spend the greater part of his life in America.

Praise for The Path

"The Path *is a deeply moving revelation of one man's poignant search for truth. With this book, Walters provides us with a rarely seen portrait of the joys and the problems of the spiritual path.* The Path *is filled with profound insight and practical advice for the novice and the more advanced seeker. I cannot conceive of anyone not deriving value from reading Walters' life story."*

—Michael Toms, Founder and President,
New Dimensions Radio
*"This book let me see inside the life and teaching of a great modern
saint. Yogananda has found a worthy Boswell to convey not only the
man but the spirit of the man."*
—James Fadiman, author of *Unlimiting
Your Life* and *Essential Sufism*

•   •   •   •   •

In this collection of nearly two hundred stories, the remarkable
qualities are revealed with breathtaking clarity. The stories cover
a diverse range of spiritual practices and topics, presented in an
enjoyable, easy-to-read format.

Swami Kriyananda
As We Have Known Him
Asha Praver

The greatness of a spiritual teacher is only partially revealed by
the work of his own hands. The rest of the story is one he cannot tell
for himself. It is the influence of his consciousness on those who come
in contact with him—whether for a brief moment, or for a lifetime of
spiritual training. In this unusual biography, the remarkable qualities
of Swami Kriyananda himself are revealed with breathtaking clarity.

Swami Kriyananda, a foremost disciple of Paramhansa Yogananda
has been prodigious in his service to his Guru. His books and music
are available in 28 languages and 100 countries. In India, millions
of people watch his daily television show. He has founded schools,

retreats, and communities on three continents. He has circled the globe lecturing and teaching.

• • • • •

Crystal Clarity also offers an additional biographical resource about Swami Kriyananda.

Faith Is My Armor
The Life of Swami Kriyananda
Devi Novak

Faith Is My Armor tells the complete story of Swami Kriyananda's life: from his childhood in Rumania, to his desperate search for meaning in life, and to his training under his great Guru, the Indian Master, Paramhansa Yogananda. As a youth of 22, he first met and pledged his discipleship to Yogananda, entering the monastery Yogananda had founded in Southern California.

• • • • •

If you'd like a succinct, easy-to-understand overview of Yogananda's teachings and their place within ancient and contemporary spiritual thought and practices, we suggest:

God Is for Everyone

Inspired by Paramhansa Yogananda,
written by Swami Kriyananda

This book outlines the core of Yogananda's teachings. God Is for Everyone presents a concept of God and spiritual meaning that will appeal to everyone, from the most uncertain agnostic to the most fervent believer. Clearly and simply written, thoroughly nonsectarian and non-dogmatic in its approach, with a strong emphasis on the underlying unity of all religions, this is the perfect introduction to the spiritual path.

Praise for God Is for Everyone

"This book makes accessible the inspired pursuit of Bliss in simple, understandable ways. Written as an introduction for those just starting on the spiritual path, it is also a re-juvenating and inspiring boost for experienced seekers. Clear, practical techniques are offered to enhance personal spiritual practices. The author maintains that "everyone in the world is on the spiritual path" whether they know it or not, even if they are temporarily merely seeking pleasure and avoiding pain. Sooner or later, "They will want to experience Him (God)." Experiencing God—and specifically experiencing God as Bliss—is that underlying goal of this work, based on the teachings of a self-realized teacher. It hits the mark for contemporary spirituality."

—*ForeWord Magazine*

•   •   •   •   •

Crystal Clarity also makes available many music and audio-book resources. Here are some that you might find helpful:

AUM: Mantra of Eternity • Swami Kriyananda

This recording features nearly 70 minutes of continuous vocal chanting of AUM, the Sanskrit word meaning peace and oneness of spirit.

Gayatri Mantra • Swami Kriyananda

This Mantra is one of the most revered of all Vedic mantras. The mantra helps bring about a Divine awakening of the mind and soul.

Mahamrityanjaya Mantra • Swami Kriyananda

The Mahamrityunjaya mantra reflects the soul's call for enlightenment through the practice of purifying ones karma—and soul.

Ananda Kirtan Chanting Series • Ananda Kirtan

These CDs contain live group chanting versions of most of the best-known and loved chants written by Paramhansa Yogananda and Swami Kriyananda. Preformed by Ananda Kirtan, and accompanied by guitar, harmonium, kirtals and tabla.

Kriyananda Chants Yogananda • Swami Kriyananda

Hear Swami Kriyananda chant the spiritualized songs of his guru, Paramhansa Yogananda, in a unique and deeply inward way.

Crystal Clarity Publishers

Crystal Clarity Publishers—recognized worldwide for its bestselling, original, unaltered edition of Paramhansa Yogananda's classic *Autobiography of a Yogi*—offers many additional resources to assist you in your spiritual journey including over ninety books, a wide variety of inspirational and relaxation music composed by Swami Kriyananda, Yogananda's direct disciple, and yoga and meditation DVDs.

For our online catalog, complete with secure ordering, please visit us on the web at:

www.crystalclarity.com

Crystal Clarity music and audiobooks are available on all the popular online download sites. Look for us on your favorite online music website.

To request a catalog, place an order for the products you read about in the *Further Explorations* section of this book, or to find out more information about us and our products, please contact us:

Crystal Clarity Publishers
14618 Tyler Foote Road
Nevada City, CA 95959

800.424.1055 or 530.478.7600
fax: 530.478.7610
email: clarity@crystalclarity.com